Coping with

MENTAL ILLNESS

Barbara Moe

The Rosen Publishing Group, Inc.
New York

This book is dedicated to all those who struggle with mental illness.

Published in 2001 by The Rosen Publishing Group, Inc.
29 East 21st Street, New York, NY 10010

First Edition

Cover photo ©Telegraph Colour Library/FPG

Library of Congress Cataloging-in-Publication Data

Moe, Barbara A.
    Coping with mental illness / by Barbara Moe. — 1st ed.
        p.   cm.
    Includes bibliographical references and index.
    ISBN: 978-1-4358-8652-0
        1. Mental illness—Juvenile literature. 2. Schizophrenia—
Juvenile literature. [1. Mental illness.] I. Title.
    RC460.2 .M64 2000
    616.89—dc21

                                                        00-009904

Manufactured in the United States of America

About the Author

Barbara Moe, R.N., M.S.N., M.S.W., is a nurse, social worker, and writer with an interest in helping young people conquer life's challenges. She is the author of several books, including *Coping with Tourette Syndrome and Tic Disorders, Coping with Eating Disorders, Coping as a Survivor of a Violent Crime, Coping with PMS, Coping with Bias Incidents,* and *Coping with Chronic Illness.*

Acknowledgments

I appreciate the help of Susan Armitage, R.N.; David Burgess, M.S.W.; Sara Grote; Amy Moe, M.S.W.; David Moe; Paul Moe, M.D.; Steve Moe, M.D.; Laurie Sorotkin; and Melanie Tem, M.S.W. Special thanks to David Coy, Mark, Samantha, and all of the other consumers who shared their stories.

Contents

Introduction

November 21, 1999. The headline of Denver's *Rocky Mountain News* reads, "Colorado's Dark Secret." The secret: The state mental hospital sterilized patients for more than thirty years. But sadly, this is not a problem just in Colorado. The newspaper article states: "Nationwide, tens of thousands of people, mostly mentally ill women, were sterilized prior to the 1970s under state laws that were upheld by the United States Supreme Court." One of these young women, only seventeen years old at the time and considered mentally ill, is now seventy-five. She says, "They got away with murder. They took out my heart and left a stone."

People today shake their heads at this injustice. "That was a long time ago," they say. "Things are different now."

Attitudes may have changed in the last fifty years, but there are still many misconceptions about the causes and treatments for mental illness. Consider the hit movie *Shine,* in which Geoffrey Rush played the part of professional pianist David Helfgott, who was an Australian with schizophrenia. The movie portrays David's father, Peter, as a mean, violent man, perhaps wrongly implying that Peter caused David's mental illness. David's oldest sister, Margaret, presents another way of looking at the situation in her 1998 book, *Out of Tune: David Helfgott and the Myth of* Shine. In the book she points out the hereditary roots of

1

David's illness: A paternal aunt spent many years of her adult life in a mental institution. Although no one really knows what caused his mental illness, one thing is certain: David Helfgott had pain in his life, but he also had joy and success.

Many famous people have had mental health problems: political figures Abraham Lincoln and Winston Churchill, artists Vincent van Gogh and Michelangelo, writers Edgar Allan Poe and William Styron, poet Sylvia Plath, composer Ludwig van Beethoven, actresses Vivian Leigh and Patty Duke, scientist Isaac Newton, media giant Ted Turner, and television newsman Mike Wallace.

Then there's Martha, an ordinary woman. After a short career as a teacher, she married a family doctor and raised three daughters, all of whom have children of their own. Medications that control Martha's bipolar disorder make her shake so much she has to hold a cup or a glass with both hands. The shaking and Martha's halting speech give acquaintances a clue that something isn't quite right. But it's a "don't ask don't tell" policy with Martha. She doesn't mention her mental illness because she isn't sure that people will be accepting of her condition. And because most people are embarrassed to pry, they don't often bother asking Martha what is wrong.

Even at the beginning of the new millennium, shrouds of shame and secrecy hide Martha's mental illness. She is not alone. Many people do not feel comfortable admitting that they have a mental illness, not even to themselves.

Bringing mental illness out of the closet is one of the goals of this book. For most of history, society has shunned people with mental illness. Even today, mental illnesses carry a stigma. But, as we will see, mental illnesses are conditions with a chemical, environmental, or biological base just like any other disease. And with the growing amount of information doctors and mental health practitioners have about different mental illnesses, they are better able to treat those who suffer from these ailments. Today, many people with mental illness are able to lead normal, productive lives. The more each of us understands about these diseases and how to deal with them, the easier it will be for those who are affected to lead healthy, happy lives.

It is important to become familiar with some of the terminology used in the mental health world; some of these terms will be used throughout this book. For instance, instead of calling themselves "patients," like those who have physical ailments, people receiving treatment for mental illnesses, or mental disorders, like to speak of themselves as "consumers." They consume mental health services. Also, in this book we will most often use the term "mental illness," but you may also hear the terms "mental disorder," "mental health problem," or "mental disturbance." A newer term that you may see in other materials written about the subject is "neuro-biologic disorder" (NBD).

This book will concentrate on two common types of mental illness: (1) mood disorders, major depression, and bipolar disorder; and (2) schizophrenia, which affects 1 out of every 100 people in the United States. It will also cover some other mental conditions that are typically less severe but still potentially disabling. They are anxiety disorders, such as panic disorder and obsessive-compulsive disorder (OCD). Keep in mind, these are only a few—though they are the most common—of the numerous mental illnesses that affect people. If you wish to learn about mental illnesses that are not discussed here, you can refer to the *Diagnostic and Statistical Manual of Mental Disorders,* a book created by the American Psychiatric Association, which gives information about hundreds of mental disorders. It is the resource that mental health practitioners use to diagnose the consumers they treat.

By reading this book, you will learn when and how to get help for yourself and others, and learn about the variety of mental health providers available, about the different kinds of therapy, and how treatment works. By the time you finish, you will understand that there is hope for those suffering with mental illness.

About Mental Illness

Everyone wants to have good mental health. Those who do have good mental health most of the time:

- ⮑ Feel happy and relaxed

- ⮑ Feel at peace with themselves

- ⮑ Feel comfortable with others

- ⮑ Believe they can meet life's challenges

And yet, no sharp dividing line exists between those with good mental health and those with a mental illness. No one is happy and content all of the time.

Mental Illness or Bad Hair Day?

Maybe you've heard someone say, "So-and-so isn't herself lately." Maybe you've made a similar comment about yourself: "I just don't feel like myself recently." What does "yourself" feel like anyway?

John's "self" is shy. He hates big parties, especially his parents' annual holiday brunch. He doesn't want to appear at this event; he doesn't want to answer the adults' questions about what he's going to do with his life. He doesn't know. He doesn't want to hear his parents' friends suggest that he take out their daughter Lisa. John doesn't feel ready to date and doesn't have much money.

John sometimes gets "bogged down" by evening; he likes to plop in front of the television for a while. By the next morning he feels better. He gets up early and runs three miles. Then he comes home, takes a shower, and eats three bowls of cereal.

This is John when he is "himself."

However, in the last few weeks, John has gone to bed at 7 PM. He doesn't do his homework and doesn't watch television. Barely able to get out of bed in the morning, he has also given up jogging and showering. His appetite has decreased and he often goes to school without breakfast.

John is currently not "himself." John may be sliding into depression and may even have a mental illness. If this state of mind continues, John should seek help.

Some people go for a long time without feeling like themselves. They may have had losses in their lives, such as a death, the breakup of a relationship, or a move to a new city. After a period of time, they start to feel better. They have had a depression based on sad events, but they do not have a mental illness. Other people, however, are depressed for long periods of time for no apparent reason. These people may be suffering from mental illness and may benefit from treatment.

What Is Mental Illness?

A recent report by the Surgeon General of the United States says that one in every five Americans experiences mental illness in any given year. Half of all Americans have such a disorder at some time in their lives.

A mental illness is a brain disorder that seriously affects a person and his or her relationships with others. Mental illness disrupts people's moods, perceptions, thoughts, and behaviors. Doctors believe that many mental illnesses have a chemical basis. Treatment can help a person with a mental illness in the same way that treatment helps people who are sick with other types of diseases. Like other illnesses, mental health problems need to be treated as soon as possible, otherwise they may get harder and harder to cope with or cure.

John continued feeling depressed for several months. It got to the point where his grades were dropping dramatically, he was losing weight, and he had no desire to leave the house.

Eventually, he got help. To keep his symptoms in check, he now takes daily medication. He tries to keep his consumption of burgers and fries to a minimum, to sleep well but not too much, and to go for his daily run. With the help of his psychiatrist, John has begun working on healthy ways to deal with stress. Several of John's relatives on his father's side (an uncle and two cousins) also have a major depressive disorder. "It's nice to know I'm not alone," John says with a wry smile.

While a mental illness is like other illnesses in many ways, it is also different. One difference is that a person with a mental illness goes to a psychiatrist, a doctor who specializes in treating mental disorders. The psychiatrist makes a diagnosis, and by doing so gives a name to the disorder.

Psychosis: What Is It?

Psychosis means loss of touch with reality. Some people think that psychosis is the same as mental illness, but this is not true. Psychosis can be a symptom of mental illness. It may involve hallucinations (such as hearing voices when no one is talking), having delusions (false beliefs), or both. Not everyone with a mental illness gets psychotic or has a "psychotic break." A psychotic break may be very short, but when it happens, it's scary for everyone involved. Psychotic breaks can also be frightening because they are hard to predict and can happen at any time. Psychosis may occur in any severe mental illness, including major depression, bipolar disorder, and schizophrenia. Sometimes people become psychotic for no apparent reason.

What Is Anxiety?

Anxiety is a fear or dread of something bad that could happen. Truly, there is no end to the number of things that could happen to people—car accidents, fatal diseases, germ warfare, nuclear holocaust. But most people are able to put these worries aside and go on with their lives.

Yet everyone does get anxious from time to time. A big exam, a blind date, a speech—all of these can cause anxiety. Usually, though, when the anxiety-producing event is over, the anxiety disappears. And some anxiety is actually useful. The anxiety you have before your big exam can help you study and work hard during the test. Anxiety about driving in traffic will keep you alert to dangers.

But when anxiety becomes overwhelming and lasts for half a year, a year, or even longer, it becomes a mental disorder in its own right. An anxiety disorder may go along with another mental illness, such as major depression, bipolar disorder, or schizophrenia. People with a mental illness may feel anxious because they feel a lack of control or a fear of not knowing what might happen from one day to the next or over a lifetime.

Severe anxiety can keep people from going to school and work. It can keep them from getting things done and having fun. Anxiety increases the risk of alcoholism and other drug addictions. It can also cause a variety of physical problems.

The following are some of the most common types of anxiety disorders.

Generalized Anxiety Disorder (GAD)

GAD may accompany other mental disorders. Symptoms include trouble sleeping, tiring easily, a feeling of restlessness and distractibility, irritability, and muscle tension. Even young children can have a generalized anxiety disorder.

Tom's father died when Tom was nine years old. For years before his death, Tom's father had had recurrences of his cancer. Tom, always a quiet child, believes his anxiety disorder started during his father's illness.

Panic Disorder

Panic attacks combine irrational fears with sudden bursts of physical symptoms that make people think they are having a heart attack or are dying. Panic attacks usually start when someone is a teenager or in his or her early twenties. Some people have only one panic attack in their lifetime; others have them on a regular basis. Some people say that the worst part of suffering from a panic attack is the anxiety about having another one. Although many people do not know what causes their panic attacks to happen, doctors have determined that some behaviors, like substance abuse, may contribute to panic attacks.

"When I was a senior in high school," says Vicki, "I drank like a fish. Pardon the expression. I was just so stressed out about my grades, and it helped me relax. Then I started getting these really scary symptoms. For no particular reason, at no particular time, my heart would start to pound. I would shake and sweat, get short of breath, feel sick to my stomach, and have this tight feeling in my chest. I thought I was having a heart attack, but my doctor said people my age don't have heart attacks. When I stopped drinking and learned how to manage my stress with breathing exercises and by working out regularly, I stopped having panic attacks."

Phobias

Phobias come in many varieties. Phobias are irrational fears of social situations or of specific places (e.g., claustrophobia—fear of being closed in) or of things (e.g., arachnophobia—fear of spiders). Agoraphobia is the anxiety disorder that often goes along with panic attacks. A person with agoraphobia fears being in public places or away from the safety of his or her home.

Post-Traumatic Stress Disorder (PTSD)

Post-traumatic stress disorder is a combination of symptoms that a person may experience after a tragic and overwhelming negative experience, such as a rape, witnessing domestic violence, being involved in a serious vehicle crash, or a natural disaster. The person may feel "numb," have flashbacks of the event, be unable to sleep or concentrate, and have fears of certain people and places.

Obsessive-Compulsive Disorder (OCD)

Obsessive-compulsive disorder involves having obsessions (repetitive, persistent thoughts that the mind cannot seem to get rid of) and compulsions (repetitive behaviors done in response to those thoughts). Experts believe OCD is hereditary.

Joe is the last one to leave his house every morning. He is often late for school because he has to change his clothes several times before the sleeves of his shirt feel "just right." He sometimes stays in the shower for thirty minutes until he feels totally clean. Finally, he often runs back into the house several times to make sure he has disconnected all of the electrical appliances.

The Biopsychosocial Model of Mental Illness

Approximately twenty-three years ago, psychiatrist George L. Engel provided us with a way of trying to understand mental illness—the biopsychosocial model. This has become the model that most, but not all, mental health workers use when examining those with mental disorders.

To better understand this concept and how doctors use it to treat consumers, we need to divide the term into three parts: bio-psycho-social. "Bio,"refers to the biological factors in mental illness, including the processes of one's brain chemistry as well as influences of one's genetic makeup, or hereditary factors. In order to treat this aspect of someone's mental disorder, doctors use medication, education, exercise, and nutrition.

"Psycho" refers to a person's psychological traits; his or her thoughts and feelings. Counseling and support groups aid in the treatment of this aspect of mental illness.

"Social" pertains to all of the outside or environmental influences on a person's life. When treating people, counselors need to consider these influences, which include a person's culture, home life, and religion.

Ouch! I Have a Pain in My Personality

Disturbances
Physical illnesses affect body organs. A headache hurts the head. A cold affects the nose and throat. Pneumonia

hurts the lungs. Mental illness hurts the personality and affects a person in many different ways.

Thoughts

People with a mental illness may have problems thinking logically, concentrating, or remembering things. They may get easily confused.

Moods

A mood is a person's state of mind, the way he or she feels at any given time. Those with a mental illness often feel either down or overly excited and hyper for an extended period of time. Some may even cycle rapidly from one mood to another for no apparent reason.

Perceptions

Perceptions are the ways in which people interpret the world around them. The way people who are suffering from mental illness perceive the world often becomes skewed. The five senses (seeing, hearing, smelling, tasting, and touching) may confuse or misinterpret information. Some people see or hear things that aren't there. They have visual or auditory hallucinations. Others feel off balance or "spacey." Still others may suffer from paranoia, thinking that people are out to get them.

Behaviors

Actions result from thoughts, moods, and perceptions. If these are "off," unusual behaviors will result. Behaviors may vary from aggressive, in-your-face types of actions to total withdrawal from life.

Mental Illness: Debunking the Myths

Myth: *There is no such thing as a mental illness.*

Fact: Yes, there is. Experts say one in five people has a mental illness at some time in his or her life.

Myth: *Mental illnesses are caused by poor parenting, lack of communication in a family, character flaws, or demon possession.*

Fact: No one knows exactly what causes mental illnesses. Most experts believe in a combination of several factors, including brain chemistry, inherited predisposition, and environmental stressors.

Myth: *Mental illness runs in families, so if your mom or dad has it, you're going to get it, too.*

Fact: The tendency to develop a mental illness does seem to run in families. Your genes (biologic units of heredity) determine which characteristics you inherit from your parents and other relatives. You may inherit an abnormal gene from your parent, but you may not.

Myth: *People with mental illnesses are very dangerous.*

Fact: People with mental illnesses may be unpredictable (just like many people without mental illness), but they are usually not dangerous, especially if they are receiving treatment.

Myth: *Mental hospitals are bad places, "loony bins" for "psychos," and people should avoid them.*

Fact: A mental hospital can be a supportive place for someone in an acute phase of a mental illness. These days most hospital stays are short but are usually helpful and stabilizing.

Myth: *People who talk about suicide won't go through with it.*

Fact: People who talk about suicide often do go through with it. Anyone who hears another person talk about suicide should treat the threat very seriously and should assist the person in getting help.

Myth: *Once you have a mental illness, you will always have a mental illness.*

Fact: Some mental illnesses cannot be totally cured, but most respond positively to treatment and are kept under control. Some even go away.

Getting Help

It's often hard for people to admit they need help and to ask for it. For example, people who suffer from migraine headaches may treat themselves with over-the-counter painkillers, or they may suffer in silence for years. Some go to a doctor for help, but many do not.

It's the same with mental illness. Even under pressure from parents, school, or courts, many young people with mental illnesses resist help.

"I'm not crazy!" Bob shouts at his mother. "Maybe you're crazy. Maybe you should go see a doctor!" Bob's angry outburst shows he's not ready to accept the idea that he needs help. Experts say that many of those who do see a professional because of symptoms of mental illness do not accept the diagnosis, at least not at first.

"I fought it," says Jake. "I was about six years old when my parents first took me to a therapist. They said I seemed unhappy. The counselor saw me twice and told my parents, 'He's just conning you.' That was the end of that.

"I was kind of a mess in high school, but therapy was uncool. In my first year of college, I could tell I needed help. The first guy I saw put me on some

medication that gave me diarrhea, so I quit taking it and didn't go back. I dropped out of college because of depression. Now I'm seeing a therapist I like and taking a low-dose antidepressant. I wish I could have gotten the help I needed a lot earlier."

Kate tells a different story. Few people are as open about their depression and mental health needs as she is. At eighteen she participated in a panel discussion for mental health professionals. "I've been in therapy almost my whole life," says Kate. "Ever since I was adopted at age seven, I've gone every week. Sometimes my parents come into the session with me. I'm doing pretty well, and I'm grateful for the help I do receive."

People from all backgrounds go to therapists, counselors, psychologists, and psychiatrists. For some people, it's the fashionable thing to do. For others, it's a life-or-death matter. Getting help is not shameful. It's sensible and useful. If you find yourself asking, "What will people think?" ask yourself a couple of other questions. What will people think if you're always down on yourself and no fun to be around? What will they think if you do something harmful to yourself or others?

Confidentiality

Before you go to a therapist, it's important to understand confidentiality. Confidentiality means your therapist will not reveal what you say in session to your parents or other adults no matter how much these adults would like to know what you're thinking and saying. However, if you state the intent to kill yourself (suicide) or others (homicide), the therapist cannot keep this information secret.

Do You Need Help? A Mental Health Test

You may have some of the following warning signs without having a serious mental illness. But if these symptoms drag on for a long time and disrupt your daily life, you may need help.

- You can't make decisions.

- You feel very lonely.

- You feel like crying, or you cry a lot.

- Everything you can think of to do seems boring.

- You feel unhappy most of the time.

- You get angry over little things or blow up for no reason.

- You don't have satisfying relationships.

- You feel so low that you can barely move, or you feel so high you can't stop moving.

- You can't sleep, or you sleep all the time.

- Your family members and/or friends have commented on your behavior. They say they're worried about you.

➷ You have used substances, such as nicotine, alcohol, and/or illegal drugs to treat your depression, to calm you down, to help you sleep, or as a way to escape.

➷ You find yourself thinking you have no particular reason for living, that your family and friends would be better off without you.

What to Do Next

Maybe you answered yes to several of the above questions and you think that you may be suffering from a mental illness. Then what? Maybe you're ready to consider getting help, but you don't know where to start.

Your Primary Doctor

Most young people have seen a doctor at some time in the past. This person may have been a family doctor or a pediatrician. Most health care programs require that you see your primary doctor before you see a psychiatrist. Your primary doctor may know a lot about mental illness and be able to help you. Or, he or she may refer you to a psychiatrist, a specialist in the diagnosis and treatment of mental illness.

Finding Out What's Wrong

In making a diagnosis of mental illness, the doctor will depend on you. Why? Because as yet, there is no simple blood test or X ray to help in making a mental illness diagnosis. The doctor has to rely on your honesty as you describe your symptoms, past illnesses, and family history.

However, the doctor may use certain blood tests to rule out physical causes (such as a malfunctioning thyroid gland) for symptoms. To rule out other medical illness as a cause of your symptoms, the psychiatrist or another doctor will also probably do a physical exam and a urine test.

When you first go to the doctor, try to get your parents, a trusted adult, or other relative to come with you. There are at least three good reasons for you to have someone else with you.

First, your parents and relatives can help you answer the doctor's questions about what conditions run in your family. For example, they may know that a great-grand-mother wrestled with depression her entire life or that your uncle suffers from a panic disorder.

Second, it's hard for any of us to remember our behaviors when we were younger—or to be objective about our behaviors today. If you do have a mental illness, you may have distortions in your thinking and perceptions. A parent or trusted adult can serve as an objective person who can perhaps more accurately describe your behavior.

A third reason for bringing along a trusted adult is that there are many questions you should ask the doctor. If you feel reluctant to ask, they can help with questions such as:

↶ Do you like working with young people?

↶ Do you think you can help us? (It's your mental illness, of course, but it does affect the family.)

↶ How do you think you can help us? (The doctor won't know the exact answer to this question right now but probably can give you a general idea.)

⇔ How much experience have you had? What is your philosophy about treating mental illness?

⇔ What do you believe about medication and other types of therapy? Do you use group therapy? Family therapy?

⇔ How often will we need to come? How long is each session?

⇔ How far in advance would we have to change or cancel an appointment?

⇔ Do you accept phone calls outside of regularly scheduled appointments?

⇔ How much do you charge and what will be the arrangements for payment?

⇔ How long do you think treatment will last?

Also, you might want to ask yourself the following:

⇔ Do I want a male or female therapist?

⇔ Do I want an older therapist or a younger one?

The Doctor's Questions

The doctor will also have many questions to ask you. Try to be patient. Your answers about your relationships, moods, thoughts, perceptions, behaviors, and possible substance abuse are important. The more your doctor knows about you, the more he or she can help.

You may feel that some of the questions the doctor asks are embarrassing or too personal. If you don't feel comfortable answering these questions in front of your parents, it's okay to ask to speak to the doctor alone. For example, many young people would feel uncomfortable discussing sexual activity, substance abuse, or homosexuality in front of their parents. If you prefer, you might ask to start the first interview with just you and the mental health professional.

Here is a sample of the types of questions your doctor may ask about your personal and family history.

- Has anyone in your family, including parents or grandparents, had a mental illness? Which ones? Did the person take medication for the mental illness? What did he or she take? Was the person ever hospitalized for mental illness? Did anyone in the family ever attempt suicide? Do any other illnesses run in your family?

- How about you? Did a doctor ever tell you that you have a mental illness? Which mental illness? Have you taken medication for it?

- What other medications do you take or have you taken? For what conditions do you take these medications?

- Have you ever used alcohol or street drugs, such as marijuana, amphetamines, cocaine, or others? Which drugs are you using now and how much are you taking? How often?

⮑ Do you have any allergies to drugs, food, or other substances?

⮑ What are the major stresses in your life right now?

The Mental Status Exam (MSE)

Sometimes, even for an experienced physician, making a diagnosis of mental illness is difficult. In order to come up with an accurate diagnosis, the doctor needs to get as much information as possible. That's why in addition to the physical examination and an inquiry into your family and personal history, the doctor will perform a mental status exam.

The mental status exam is not a formal "test." In fact, most of the mental status exam will probably feel like a chat with the doctor, who bases some of his or her conclusions on observation. The doctor will make note of the following:

1) General Description or Presentation
Appearance
Are you taking good care of yourself? Are your clothes clean and reasonably neat? Is your hair combed?

Behavior
Are you pacing the floor? Do you sit or stand straight or slumped over? Do you move slowly? Are you restless?

Attitude Toward the Examiner
How do you relate to the person testing you? Are you friendly and cooperative? Or are you angry and defensive?

A doctor describes Michael in this way: "The most notable thing about Michael's mental status exam is how he relates to the examiner. He is quite distant and rather mechanical. Little warmth emanates from him, and the feeling in the room is one of a lack of interpersonal chemistry."

2) Speech

⇒ Do you talk very fast?

⇒ Do you talk a lot and interrupt frequently?

⇒ Do you hardly talk at all?

⇒ Do you tend to mumble?

⇒ Do you speak only when spoken to?

3) Mood and Affect

Mood refers to the way you feel. It is a reflection of your mental state at any given time. Are you mainly sad and feel like there's no reason for living? Does your mood change from one hour to the next?

Affect refers to the way you come across to others. Some people appear to have no emotions. They don't cry, smile, frown, or change their expression. Doctors say these people have a flat affect. Other people may have an angry affect, an anxious affect, or a happy affect.

Michael's doctor says, "He presents dramatic or upsetting information in a matter-of-fact way. His affect is bland and does not change. Over the course of an hour evaluation, he never showed anger nor did he ever smile."

The doctor will also note the appropriateness of your emotions. If your grandmother died last week and you can't stop laughing, the doctor may consider your mood and affect inappropriate to the situation.

4) Perceptions

Perceptions relate to the way you view the world. What one person perceives as pleasure, another may perceive as pain. For example, climbing a mountain may be fun for you but terrifying for someone else. Abnormal perceptions are a common trait of mental illness, often having to do with disturbances of the five senses, especially hearing and seeing. Hallucinations, or seeing things that aren't there, are examples of disturbances in perception.

5) Thoughts

Doctors often divide thoughts into two categories. One category is thought processes, or the way you put ideas together. For example, do your thoughts race and jump from one subject to another? Or are your thoughts sluggish and slow? Do you answer the question asked, or do you start talking about a subject not related to the question?

The other category has to do with what you are actually thinking. Do you have delusions (false beliefs)? Do you have thoughts of suicide? Do you have homicidal thoughts? Are you paranoid, constantly thinking everyone is talking about you or out to get you?

Michael says he has had lots of "weird vibes." Recently he has become excessively self-conscious and is prone to dwell on worries, especially that people are talking about him or thinking badly of him. Frequently when he enters a room, people give him dirty looks, he says.

6) Cognitions

Cognitions also relate to brain functioning. This part of the mental status exam assesses your intelligence and knowledge of the world, your mental alertness, your memory, your ability to concentrate, your ability to do abstract thinking, and your judgment and insight.

- Intelligence and knowledge of the world: Do you know who the president of the United States is? Do you know who the first president was? Do you know how far it is to California from your home?

- Mental alertness and orientation: What is your name, address, and telephone number? What is the date and time? What is the name of the place in which we are meeting?

- Memory: Can you talk about your childhood? Can you recall three important news stories of the past month? What did you have for lunch yesterday? What did you have for breakfast today? Can you look at a tray containing five items and remember them five minutes later?

↪ Concentration: Can you subtract 7 from 100 and keep subtracting sevens? If not, can you subtract threes from fifty? How about your multiplication tables? Do you remember the product of 7 x 7?

↪ Abstract thinking: To test your ability to deal with concepts, the doctor may ask questions such as: What are the differences between an apple and an orange? Can you interpret the meaning of "People who live in glass houses shouldn't throw stones" or the statement "Even monkeys fall from trees."

7) Judgment and Insight

Your ability to make sound judgments and decisions will also be tested. The doctor may ask questions such as, "What would you do if you smelled smoke in your house?"

Insight refers to your understanding and acceptance of your mental illness.

Michael's doctor wrote this in his report: "He spoke of his desire to be in charge of the world so that he could get what he wants. However, there was no sense that Michael had any insight that this was an unreasonable wish."

8) Substance Abuse

The doctor will ask if you use alcohol or illegal drugs. Many people with mental illnesses use these substances. They use them to self-medicate, to try to numb or kill the pain of living. It's important to give honest answers to these questions even if you need to ask your parents to leave during this part of the interview.

Hannah, an eighteen-year-old young woman, dropped out of high school in her senior year. Her doctor's report reads: "Hannah admits to drinking a lot and enjoying the use of drugs. Her drinking tends to be in flurries. She admits to drinking four or five beers a night during the week and more on weekends. She typically does not drink when in one of her high states because when she is in that state, alcohol simply does not affect her.

"Hannah has used marijuana heavily in the past but discovered that marijuana made her feel paranoid. She no longer uses it at all. She has also used acid. She has tried cocaine when it was available but does not seek it out. One of her friends was on Ritalin, so she tried that drug, which made her feel high. Occasionally she uses over-the-counter stimulants.

"Hannah says she 'smokes like a fiend.' She used to smoke two packs a day but now, because of cost concerns, she rolls her own cigarettes and smokes the equivalent of a pack a day." The doctor concluded that Hannah's drug use had an effect on her mental illness.

After the doctor has finished with testing, he or she will write a report. The doctor will make recommendations for treatment or may suggest further testing.

One part of the report may look mysterious but really isn't. This is the five-scale or five-axis classification set out in the American Psychiatric Association's *Diagnostic and Statistical Manual of Mental Disorders*. The main reason for its development was to standardize psychiatric diagnoses. It can also be used by third-party payers, such as insurance companies, or for research studies. Most important for you, it is used to create a detailed diagnosis that will determine how your illness is treated.

 ➷Axis I: This consists of illnesses that "come on you," such as bipolar disorder or schizophrenia.

 ➷Axis II: This line includes experiences that have "traveled with you," such as childhood abuse.

 ➷Axis III: On this line the doctor records any physical conditions you might have, such as epilepsy or diabetes. These may or may not have something to do with the mental illness.

 ➷Axis IV: This section refers to the level of stress in your life. A rating of one indicates low stress; a rating of six indicates a very high level of stress.

 ➷Axis V: On this line the doctor estimates how well you have functioned in the previous year. Here a high number, such as ninety, indicates a high functioning level. A low number, such as five, indicates a low level of functioning in the world.

Even after comprehensive testing, the doctor may not be absolutely sure of a diagnosis and may need to see you again.

Mental Health Professionals

We call psychiatrists, psychologists, social workers, family therapists, psychiatric nurses, and case managers mental health professionals. All are dedicated to helping those with mental illnesses achieve the best possible mental health. Two terms you may hear in connection with mental health professionals are "licensed" and "certified." A licensed professional has met state requirements and passed a test given by an examining board. A certified mental health professional has met the standards of a professional organization, a state or national organization, or has completed specialized training. The words "therapist," "psychotherapist," and "counselor" are generic words that various people can use to describe themselves. Check qualifications and credentials carefully.

The following is a list of the various different types of mental health professionals you are likely to encounter.

- Psychiatrists are medical doctors who have completed medical school plus several years of residency training. They are certified when they pass the examination of the American Board of Psychiatry and Neurology. Psychiatrists are the only mental health professionals who can prescribe medication and order medical tests. They will have the initials "M.D." after their name.

- Psychologists are "doctors of psychology." They have earned a doctorate degree, or Ph.D. They practice psychotherapy and do mental testing.

- Licensed clinical social workers may practice psychotherapy. They have a master's degree in social work plus extra supervised experience in counseling. Depending on what type of counseling they specialize in, they will have either the initials M.S.W. (master of social work), L.C.S.W. (licensed clinical social worker), or L.I.S.W. (licensed independent social worker) after their name.

⇌ Family therapists have at least a master's degree with additional training and supervised practice in doing therapy with families. They may be certified by their state organization and by the American Association for Marriage and Family Therapy.

⇌ Psychiatric nurses have a master's degree in psychiatric nursing in addition to a nursing degree.

⇌ Licensed professional counselors (L.P.C.s) have completed a master's degree and at least two years of postgraduate supervised practice.

⇌ Case managers are people who work to coordinate services for people with a mental illness. They may have professional degrees in psychology, counseling, nursing, or social work. Or they may have had on-the-job experience helping people get psychiatric help, medical care, vocational training, independent living skills, and help in crisis situations.

Where Do People Get Treatment for Mental Illnesses?

People get treatment for mental illnesses in a number of different settings. Most go for therapy to a doctor's office, a clinic, or a mental health center. Sometimes people need the more intensive services of a day treatment program; they spend the day at the facility and return home at night. Hospitals, residential treatment centers, boarding homes, and skilled nursing facilities offer twenty-four-hour care. Some consumers need help on a regular basis but can function without constant supervision. For these individuals, the help of assisted independent living programs with on-site or off-site counselors allows them to try independent living without all of the stress associated with being completely on their own. Assisted living programs do differ from each other a great deal, but in essence they all attempt to give consumers as much freedom as possible while providing needed support and supervision.

Getting help for a mental illness and keeping it under control are not simple processes. But they will be worth the effort and can prevent an easily treatable problem from worsening into a debilitating, life-long illness.

Mental Illness:
What Works?

Treatment for mental illness works. But not all treatments work for all people. Researchers have done hundreds of scientific studies showing the effectiveness of various treatments. Once you admit to yourself that you have a mental illness, you'll be that much closer to getting help. But what kind of treatment is available and which will work best for you?

Let's go back to the biopsychosocial model of looking at mental illness. In order to treat the "bio" element of your disorder, doctors prescribe medications, such as anti-depressants, to attack the presumed chemical imbalance in the brain. Many people are against the use of psychiatric medications because they equate them with mind control and being "zombielike."

Cody pointed out to his mother, "You tell me not to mess with drugs and alcohol and then some doctor says I can get better only if I take the drugs she prescribes for me. I don't see what the difference is. They both mess with my head."

Although psychiatric medications do affect the brain, they are relatively safe when taken as directed, and most do not lead to addiction. They do not, like street drugs, cause more problems than they solve. Also, they are used in combination with other therapies and under medical supervision.

Psychological treatments—which deal with the "psycho" element of a disorder—help people cope with relationships, with work or school, with issues from the past, and with environmental stressors, such as the fast pace of life in the twenty-first century. Psychological approaches to healing include "talking" therapies of all kinds and relaxation techniques.

And finally, "social" or supportive treatments help a person live in the world and include financial support, vocational help, assistance with housing, and education about mental illness.

Because each illness and each person is different, you will need to find a specialized treatment plan that works for you.

Medications

In spite of the probable benefits, few people enjoy taking pills. In fact, people's dislike of taking their prescribed medications often causes big problems for those with mental illness.

Zach is an eighteen-year-old high school senior who is currently in the hospital because of symptoms of bipolar disorder. Over the past two years, he has had two other hospitalizations because of manic episodes. In the past several weeks, Zach has spent large amounts of money he doesn't have, hasn't slept well, has called several people in the middle of the night, and believes some people are out to get him.

Zach says he doesn't see anything particularly disturbing about his behavior. He says he's proud of having lost forty-five pounds this year. He has to admit, though, that his grades in school have been dropping in recent weeks. In the hospital Zach sings loudly at all hours of the day and can't seem to stay in his room.

Over time, Zach's doctor has prescribed several medications he thought would help control Zach's symptoms. Zach says he doesn't need medication and besides, he doesn't like the side effects. Lithium makes him shake, so he can't play his guitar. Depakote, he's afraid, will cause him to gain weight. Tegretol made his eye twitch, and Lamictal made him dizzy.

Instead of giving different medications a fair trial, Zach is hanging on to his manic behaviors. He says he likes them even though he knows he won't like the depression that will come later.

Medications doctors prescribe to treat major mental illnesses include antianxiety agents, antidepressants, antipsychotics, and mood stabilizers.

All medications have a trade or brand name, as well as a chemical, generic, or scientific name. An example is the pain reliever that we call either Tylenol (brand name) or acetaminophen (chemical name). The chemical names are sometimes hard to remember, spell, and pronounce. Therefore, in this book, we will consistently use the more familiar trade name first, followed by the chemical name.

Side Effects of Medications: Options You May Have
Side effects are the unwanted effects of a medication. For example, a certain drug may help a person's mood, but he or she may find it causes sleepiness. All medications have potential side effects. Aspirin can cause stomach ulcers, and certain antibiotics can cause rashes or nausea and vomiting. Be sure to talk with your doctor in advance about possible side effects and what to do if you get them. The side effects of most medications do not affect everyone because each person's body chemistry is different. You may experience all, some, or none of the unwanted symptoms.

If you experience side effects from your medication, you may think you have only two choices: to take the medication and put up with the side effects or discontinue the drug. Actually, you have other options.

↬ Ask your doctor about changing the "timing" of your doses. For example, consider morning doses for a medication that causes insomnia. Or take a medication that causes sleepiness closer to bedtime.

↬ Ask your doctor if there are certain foods that you can eat in combination with taking your medication that will cut down on side effects.

↬ Ask your doctor if he or she can prescribe a smaller amount of the same medication.

↬ Ask your doctor about the possibility of more frequent doses of less medication each time.

⮡ Ask your doctor if you could try a different medication.

⮡ Ask your doctor if he or she could add another medication to reduce side effects.

Also, keep in mind that the intensity and frequency of side effects will change over time. Some side effects may even go away completely. It's important to keep track of all symptoms you believe are caused by your medications and let your doctor know about them.

Of course not taking pills is less expensive and less trouble than taking medication. Of course you envy your friends who don't have to worry about medications and can live a "normal" life. Of course you don't like the side effects of medication. But even if you don't realize it at first, time will probably teach you that the inconvenience and side effects are less trouble than the symptoms of your mental illness. You may realize that taking a daily medication is a small price to pay for stability and improved mental health.

Getting the Most from Your Medications

The past thirty years have seen an explosion in the number of medications used to help relieve symptoms of mental illness. That's good news for you. By using some of the medication tips below, you can help your doctor help you.

He or she will attempt to make a good match between the category of your symptoms and the class of medications. The doctor will also try to find medications for long-term treatment of your specific disorder.

Here are some dos and don'ts for medications.

Dos:

- Do expect a lag time between the time you start taking the medication and when the medication begins to make a difference. At the very least, give yourself two weeks to notice a decrease in symptoms. Four to six weeks (or even two months in some cases) is more realistic.

- Do be sure to make an effort to understand everything you can about your medication. Read the literature that comes with it. Ask your doctor about anything you don't understand.

- Do try to take your medications at the same time each day. If necessary, invent cues to help you remember. You may decide to take medications with meals or other scheduled events, use pill boxes prelabeled with dates and times, or use a timer watch.

- Do report side effects to your doctor.

- Do let your doctor know if you think you're taking too little or too much medication.

- Do remember that if you stop your medication, the side effects will go away quickly. The effects of the mental illness will take longer to reappear.

- Do be conscientious about follow-up visits to the doctor; he or she needs to carefully monitor your psychiatric medication program to make sure the frequency and size of the dosages are correct.

❧ Do learn which (if any) foods or other medications interact negatively with your mental health medications.

Don'ts:

❧ Don't stop taking your medication just because you start feeling better. Remember that your medication is probably making you feel better. Keep taking it until your doctor says you can taper down and eventually stop.

❧ Don't expect too much from a medication. Sometimes the most a person can expect is a reduction, rather than a complete disappearance, of symptoms.

❧ Don't try to adjust your medication dosage by yourself.

❧ Don't use non-prescription alternatives (herbs and nutritional supplements) without first consulting a mental health professional. They may interact badly with your medication.

Psychosocial Treatments

Psychosocial treatments refer to any kind of help for mental illness that is not medication, including talking therapies, such as one-on-one or individual counseling, group counseling, and family counseling. Which psychosocial help is offered depends on the person and his or her condition. Sometimes a person benefits from "supportive" help. Examples are tutoring for a person who is behind in school, dietary advice for someone with eating problems, or financial advice for someone who is trying to live independently. In actual therapy sessions, the counselor often combines several approaches to treatment.

There are many different psychosocial approaches to the treatment of mental illness; some of the most useful are talking therapies.

Talking Therapy

Many experts believe that medication and talking therapy go hand-in-hand and that using them in combination results in the best treatment. Talking therapy may include one-on-one meetings with a counselor, group meetings with other young people, family therapy, or learning new ways of thinking and behaving (sometimes called cognitive or behavioral therapy).

There are actually as many approaches to individual therapy as there are counselors. Sometimes it's the therapist's belief in the person's ability to heal that makes the biggest difference. The deciding factor may also come down to how much faith you have in your therapist. The relationship between you and the mental health professional is called "the helping alliance" or "the therapeutic alliance."

When you first start therapy, you and the mental health professional will talk about your goals for treatment and which approaches are likely to work best for you. Your job is to be totally honest, to reveal your thoughts, feelings, and attitudes to the therapist. The therapist's job is to help you express your feelings and problems. The professional tries to hold up a mirror for you to see yourself in ways you might otherwise not be able to see yourself. The therapist will also point out possible ways of resolving conflicts.

You will be able to tell after a couple of visits if you like the approach your therapist takes. Some counselors say very little and let you do most of the talking. Others have more of a back-and-forth, conversational approach. Some therapists are very directive, making suggestions for change and even giving "homework assignments" for you to complete between sessions.

Regardless of the approach your therapist uses, two of the main goals of psychotherapy are understanding and change. Understanding includes why you do certain things and why others do certain things. As you come to understand (to have insight), you will be kinder to yourself and to others. You may be able to let go of the shame and guilt that can accompany a diagnosis of mental illness. Change often comes from understanding.

Psychiatrist Richard M. Searles says he likes to compare individual therapy sessions to putting together a puzzle. In the early stages of therapy, the therapist and consumer together turn over the pieces that represent the various issues in the person's life. As more pieces are uncovered, the consumer and the doctor work jointly to arrange the pieces into a complete, well-put-together picture of life.

Group Therapy/Support Groups

Group therapy works well for people in certain instances. Groups help people realize that they are not alone. In group therapy, people support each other. Also, group therapy is usually less expensive than individual therapy.

If your therapist thinks you might benefit from problem solving in a group situation, give it a try. Groups meet in clinics, schools, day treatment programs, and in residential treatment settings.

In some ways, support groups are different from therapy groups but may accomplish similar goals. A professional therapist may lead your therapy group while a volunteer may lead a support group. In either situation, it's comforting to be able to open up about your illness to others who understand. You'll undoubtedly get some ideas about coping with mental illness. You'll make some new friends. A recent study showed that people with depression felt better when they believed that at least some people valued them even if they did not belong to a large number of groups or have huge numbers of friends.

There are many ways to find a support group. You can ask your doctor or other health care provider for suggestions. You can also look in the front part of your telephone book (white pages) under "Mental Health" or in the yellow pages under "Mental Health Services." Recovery, Inc., is one listing in this category. Recovery, Inc., is a twelve-step support program that follows guidelines similar to those of Alcoholics Anonymous. National mental health organizations, such as the National Alliance for the Mentally Ill (NAMI) will provide you with a listing of support groups in your area.

It's hard to go to any group for the first time. It's one thing meeting with your own counselor one-on-one. But admitting to a whole group of people that you have a mental illness takes courage.

Family Therapy/Family Support

As you have probably figured out, you are a part of many larger groups, the most intimate of which is your family. Even those who have left their family homes carry their family experiences with them.

Family therapists like to gather as many family members together as they can. However, a family therapist doesn't always work with large groups. Often it's possible to get only you and one or both parents together for a meeting.

A family therapist may teach you how to run family meetings to solve family problems outside of therapy. Some people hold family meetings at a regular time each week. Others call a family meeting when there is an issue (or issues) to discuss. Decide who will be the leader and who will be the recorder at each meeting. Below is one step-by-step example of how to proceed.

- Set up rules for the meeting. Examples might be "No name-calling" and "No opening up of old wounds."

- Define the problem. Get the input of everyone on what the main problem is, then formulate the problem in such a way that everyone can agree.

- Brainstorm for possible solutions. List everything.

- Discuss the advantages and disadvantages of each suggested solution.

- Vote on the solutions. Agree on one.

- Figure out specific plans to implement the solution.

⇌ Agree to reevaluate the solution at a specific time.

⇌ If the agreed-upon solution does not work out in a specified time, start the process over again.

Tiffany, eighteen, asked her doctor if she could be admitted to the hospital because of depression and thoughts of suicide. During her time in the hospital, she stopped feeling suicidal. However, she still wanted to drop out of school. Whenever she talked to her therapist about her parents' disappointment with her, she started to cry.

One of Tiffany's main concerns was her problems with her parents. She had frequent arguments with her mother over the mess in her room, not helping out around the house, her friends, her failing grades, failure to observe family curfews, and her pink hair and pierced tongue. Recently she had stopped taking her prescribed medication and had stolen fifty dollars from her father's sock drawer.

With the help of family therapy, Tiffany and her parents negotiated some compromises. Her parents agreed that what Tiffany did with her hair, tongue, bedroom, and school classes were her concerns. Tiffany agreed that if she wanted to continue to live at home, she would stay out of her parents' bedroom, abide by curfews, help with cooking and cleaning, and take her prescribed medications. If she dropped out of school, she would get a job and pay rent. Meanwhile, the three family members worked together to plan for Tiffany's eventual emancipation.

At a family meeting, you may learn a great deal from listening to what your parents are saying. They will certainly learn a lot from listening to you. Both sides will benefit from the help of an objective therapist.

Mental illness is sure to cause stress in a family. On the other hand, family members can provide tremendous support for each other. In order to provide support, parents need support, too. *The Bonnie Tapes* are three videos from the Mental Illness Education Project (see the Where to Go for Help section in the back of this book for contact information). In these tapes (*Mental Illness in the Family, My Sister Is Mentally Ill*, and *Recovering from Mental Illness*), Bonnie, a young woman with schizophrenia, discusses the impact of her mental illness on her family and what they did about it. Also available is the tape, *Families Coping with Mental Illness*, in which ten different family members talk about what it's like to have another family member with schizophrenia or bipolar disorder.

Cognitive Therapy

Cognition means having to do with thought processes. The basis of cognitive therapy is that stress itself does not cause bad feelings; what does cause negative feelings is how you think about yourself. A cognitive therapist will challenge negative thought patterns and help you develop ones that are positive and healthy.

(Matt comes into his therapy session with shoulders slumping, mouth set in a frown. He stares at the floor.)
Matt: Everything has gone wrong this week.

45

> *Therapist: I can't believe everything went wrong. How about telling me five things that went right.*
>
> *Matt: Well, I did get a B+ on the chemistry final. But I should have gotten an A.*
>
> *Therapist: What else went right?*
>
> *Matt: I can't think of a thing.*
>
> *Therapist: Last week you said you were going to audition for a part in the school musical. What happened?*
>
> *Matt: I didn't get a decent part. I have only about six lines.*
>
> *Therapist: Were there some people who didn't get any part at all?*
>
> *Matt: Well, sure, but . . .*

Matt's therapist knows that Matt has a strong tendency to focus on negative events more than positive ones. He is working to get Matt out of this thought pattern. Cognitive therapy is likely to help people like Matt who:

- Take responsibility for everything that goes wrong as if they are to blame for all the world's problems.

- Assume that if one thing bad happens in their day, everything else is going to go wrong.

- Think that if they make a mistake, they are bad people.

- Believe there is some standard of goodness to which they must measure up.

Behavior Therapy

Behavior, or behavioral therapy, helps a person change self-defeating actions. (In practice, cognitive and behavioral therapies are closely linked. Sometimes therapists combine them into cognitive-behavioral therapy in which they use elements from each to treat the patient.) In order to change actions that are unhealthy for you, you need to take three steps:

1. Describe the undesirable behavior.

2. Decide on your desired goal.

3. Make a commitment to yourself and change the behavior.

Let's take Brianna, who has a problem with being late. Brianna's chronic inability to get anywhere on time has cost her friends, has angered her family, and is one reason she feels bad about herself.

Following is an example of a conversation from Brianna's therapy session:

(Brianna has arrived ten minutes late for her appointment.)

Brianna: I can't get here on time. It's one of my many bad habits. I'm always late for everything.

Therapist: So what would you like to do about this?

Brianna: I really would like to get to places on time.

Therapist: You've told me several times that you have a hard time relaxing.

Brianna: True.

Therapist: In the coming week, every time you have to meet someone I want you to arrive fifteen minutes early. Bring your Walkman and listen to your

tapes while you wait. Catch the look on people's faces when they see you. Then record each one of these experiences in your journal.
   Brianna: Okay. I like that. I'll give it a try.

Although there are many ways you can change your own thinking and behavior (see chapter 6 on self-help techniques), most people need a well-trained therapist to get them started. Allow for at least twelve weekly sessions, perhaps combined with medication and other therapy to see solid results. You will also probably need to see the therapist regularly, but less frequently after that, to keep you on track.

How Do I Know If This Therapy Is Worthwhile?
It's important to evaluate your therapy every so often. While the answer to each of the following questions will not always be yes, some of them should be.

- Does my therapist seem genuinely concerned about me?

- Does my mental health professional spend most of the time on my problems rather than on his or her own stories?

- Is this person there for me in a crisis?

- Do I feel comfortable asking for advice for any problem?

- Is it okay to disagree with this person?

☙ Does the person listen when I disagree?

☙ Am I learning how to work out my own problems?

☙ Do I feel as if I am growing and changing in positive, healthy ways?

What If My Therapist Doesn't Help Me?

If you don't believe your therapist is helping you, you have every right to question what's going on. But before you seek out a different therapist, consider the following advice.

☙ Once you have found a therapist who practices the sort of therapy you prefer and whom you like, give yourself and your therapist time. No therapist can work miracles in one or even two visits. Also, if your treatment involves taking medication, remember that medication takes time to start working.

☙ Discuss your discontent with your therapist and see if you can get your therapy moving in a different direction.

How Will I Know When I Don't Need Therapy Anymore?

Most people who use mental health services long for the day when they will no longer need these services. But most people who are honest with themselves realize they may need help off and on for the rest of their lives. You, along with your parents and mental health professional, may agree that you can stop therapy if:

- ↪ You are feeling happier and more in control of your life.

- ↪ You are generally optimistic and can handle life's disappointments and losses.

- ↪ You are doing well at school and at home.

- ↪ You have supportive relationships that are working well.

- ↪ You have a better understanding of the factors that originally caused you to seek help.

Supportive Therapy

Those who have spent time in a hospital or residential treatment center will find supportive therapy one of the most important ingredients in making a successful transition back into everyday life.

Reentry into a world that everyone else takes for granted can be lonely and scary. Mental health consumers need to have the support of trained professionals to help them cope with the stresses and complications of independent living.

Jack is nineteen years old. His substance abuse problem is a direct result of his mental illness. Because of substance abuse, the police have stopped him several times for driving under the influence.

Several months ago, he lost his driver's license. Relationships with his family have become increasingly strained. Jack's parents have told him that because his behaviors negatively affect the younger children in the family, he can no longer live at home. Jack is now living on the streets.

Jack has few skills for coping with everyday life. He is not able to deal with much more than the demands that he faces as a member of the homeless community in which his primary concerns are finding a quiet place to sleep, panhandling enough money to get some food, meeting with a dealer for his drugs, and keeping out of the reach of the police. Jack needs help if he is going to make a life for himself that includes living at a residence, having a job, and having financial security. Jack also needs counseling to help him deal with his mental illness and drug addiction. Partly because of his psychotic episodes, Jack has few friends on the street, which adds to his depression.

Who will help him get an apartment? Who will help him with job skills? Who will help him learn to save his money, write checks, and use the bank or ATM? Who will help him learn to do economical grocery shopping or to eat in a restaurant and leave a tip? Who will see that he gets dental and medical checkups?

Jack is out in the world with no supports. Jack needs community support services. In addition, his parents feel horrible about their son's situation. They need support services, too.

According to the National Information Center for Children and Youth with Disabilities (NICHCY), there is a growing recognition that families need support services, often called "wrap around" services.

In his recent book, *Transforming Madness*, author Jay Neugeboren points out that people with mental illnesses need peer support, help from people like themselves who are in recovery. They need jobs, friends, and skills for living in the world—just like everyone else.

Mood Disorders

We all experience changing moods. Sometimes we're in a bad mood which makes us feel sad, sluggish, empty, or pessimistic about the future. Other times we enjoy good moods in which we feel energetic, optimistic, outgoing, and confident. Some people, however, experience these moods to great extremes. They go through periods of deep depression that last for days, weeks, or even one or more years. Some of those people also experience periods of mania. When they are manic, they are extremely happy, overly excited, and too optimistic. When people are in a manic phase, they may make choices that threaten their future or put them in physical danger.

One of the most disturbing characteristics of mood disorders is that they come and go. People with a mental illness don't know how soon or how frequently their particular mood disorder will return. But they can count on one thing: It probably will.

Doctors believe that a chemical imbalance in the brain is one of the causes of mood disorders, which include depressive and bipolar disorders.

Major Depressive Disorder

To one degree or another, depression hits everyone. Circumstances that can cause depression are the death of a loved one, a breakup of a relationship, a move to a new town, and other losses or disappointments. Even something as minor as losing a wallet can make a person feel sad and depressed for a time. Eventually, however, the sad mood lifts and the person feels like his or her normal self again.

But a major depression (sometimes called a clinical depression or unipolar depression) is more severe and lasts longer. Research shows that about 15 percent of Americans will have a major depression at least once in their lives. Your chance of a depression increases if you have had a depression before. Studies also show that depression can occur at almost any age. In fact, depression seems to be hitting people at younger and younger ages. Until adolescence, depression occurs equally in boys and girls. After adolescence, depression becomes more common in women. This trend continues into adulthood.

People with a major depression find that nothing cheers them up. The low mood may hit them for no apparent reason. It makes day-to-day functioning difficult, and it doesn't go away for a long time. In fact, the depressed mood can get so bad that the person sees no reason for living and considers suicide.

Melissa is a seventeen-year-old who came to a hospital emergency room at the urging of her psychiatrist. She had been considering killing herself either by jumping off a highway overpass or by taking a drug overdose.

Melissa had suffered from depression for most of her life. When she was younger, she started using drugs. At first they made her feel better, not exactly happy, just not depressed and miserable. Her drug use began when she was about thirteen years old, when she started using marijuana. Eventually, she and her friends started using other drugs, such as ecstasy and crystal meth. When her parents finally realized what was going on, they checked her into a drug treatment program. But coming off the drugs only added to her depression. She hated everyone, especially her parents. They had taken away the only thing that got her out of her oppressive melancholy. While she was at the treatment center, she decided she had no choice but to end her life. She took an overdose of Tylenol, which landed her in the hospital for eleven days.

She did get some treatment for her suicidal tendencies, but as soon as the doctor deemed that she was not a threat to herself, the therapy stopped. Her parents were convinced that her depression was a result of coming off of the drugs and assumed it would pass. But this would not be the case. Six months later, at the age of fifteen, she slit her wrists. After another short stay in the hospital, Melissa was admitted to a residential treatment program. It was obvious she needed intensive therapy. She stayed in that program for one and a half months—until her acute crisis period was over and she was no longer suicidal. After that, she moved to a residential program. She participated in this program for seven weeks. Finally, she moved to a boarding home/long-term psychiatric facility, in which she could learn to cope with her depression and lead a healthy, independent life. She attended this program for almost two years before deciding, against the suggestions of her doctors, to try to live on her own. She found an apartment and a job as a waitress.

At first, everything went well. Melissa loved being on her own. But then the depression started. She found herself coming home from work and crying in her dark apartment: Without a support system, she had no one to turn to and felt completely alone. She had also stopped taking her medication. She started having trouble concentrating. She was unable to remember orders that she was taking at work or which table they were supposed to go to when they came up from the kitchen. She was constantly getting yelled at by her boss, who was also on her back for showing up late almost every day. But what could she do? She was having trouble falling asleep. And when she did finally get to sleep, she had trouble getting up. She knew the symptoms of depression, but she didn't know what to do now that she was alone. She was sure that no one would understood what she was going through. This made her more depressed.

Although Melissa said she really did not want to die, she couldn't think of any other way to get rid of her symptoms.

Melissa has several symptoms common to those with major depressive disorder. They include:

☞ Trouble sleeping and feeling tired all the time. A general lack of energy. Usually feelings of low energy are worse in the morning than at any other time during the day.

☞ Trouble eating.

➪ Trouble concentrating.

➪ Overwhelming feelings of guilt for every little mistake.

➪ Desire to remain indoors and not interact with others. Complete withdrawal.

➪ Using sex and illegal drugs to self-medicate and to keep from feeling pain.

➪ Depression relapses.

➪ Suicidal tendencies.

➪ Feelings of worthlessness and despair.

➪ Failing grades or trouble at work.

➪ Feelings of loneliness.

Dysthymia

Another type of depression, called dysthymia, is less severe than major depression but is nevertheless disabling. Dysthymia describes the mood of a person who has what doctors call a low-grade depression. People with this type of depression may not even realize that something is wrong with them. They have felt sad for so long, that they don't expect anything better. They tend to eat and sleep normally but slog through their days with little joy. Experts say that some people with dysthymia have a lower quality of life than people with major depression probably because they are less likely to seek help.

Seasonal Affective Disorder (SAD)

Seasonal affective disorder (SAD) is a type of depression that typically occurs in the winter months. Much less common is a reverse type of SAD that makes people feel depressed in the summer and more energetic in winter. Seasonal affective disorder does not usually start until people are in their twenties. (Remember, though, some mood changes are normal; it is only when the depression gets disabling that a person might need to see a therapist.)

Experts say SAD affects about four times as many women as men and is more common in the northern United States. Doctors still do not know the exact causes of SAD, but there is evidence that it might be hereditary.

Treatment for SAD typically consists of exposure to bright artificial light for a period of time each day. A doctor should prescribe the "dosage" of light and type of light. The physician may also prescribe an antidepressant and suggest lifestyle changes, such as getting out in the sun and/or taking a winter vacation in a sunny climate.

Treating Depression

Therapy

Various types of psychological therapies may help with depression, especially cognitive-behavioral therapy, which was discussed in chapter 3. Through changed thoughts and changed behaviors, people find their sad moods lifting.

Another type of talking therapy is sometimes called insight-oriented therapy. In this type of therapy, a counselor helps you find reasons for some of your behaviors.

Events that happened in the past may influence how you react today. Getting insight into what happened when you were younger and reconciling those bad or painful feelings may be enough to help you change.

Interpersonal therapy, which focuses on helping people improve relationships with others, may also help.

Counselors sometimes suggest additional therapies for people in hospitals or residential treatment centers. These supplemental activities help pass the time and lift moods. They include art, music, and dance therapy.

Doctors may prescribe electroconvulsive therapy (ECT or shock treatments) for the most severe instances of depression that have not responded to other treatments. ECT is a fast-acting procedure that sends a low-voltage electrical signal through the brain while the person is anesthetized.

Doctors may suggest that you try any of the above therapies in combination with medication.

Medications

The medications most often prescribed to treat depression are called antidepressants. This category of pharmaceuticals includes selective serotonin reuptake inhibitors (SSRIs), tricyclic antidepressants, and monoamine oxidase inhibitors (MAOIs).

Doctors often prescribe SSRIs for depression. These include Prozac (fluoxetine), Zoloft (sertraline), Luvox (fluvoxamine), Paxil (paroxetine), and Celexa (citalopram). Although most people do not experience side effects from these medications, those who do most often report insomnia, nervousness, sexual problems, and gastrointestinal symptoms, such as nausea and diarrhea.

Before SSRIs were developed, doctors most often prescribed tricyclic antidepressants for depression. The most common are Elavil (amitriptyline), Tofranil (imipramine), Norpramin (desipramine), and Pamelor or Aventyl (nortriptyline). These medications may cause more troubling side effects, such as blurred vision, memory problems, dry mouth, constipation, weight gain, sleepiness, and increased heart rate.

Monoamine oxidase inhibitors (MAOIs), such as Nardil (phenelzine) and Parnate (tranylcypromine), treat depression, but doctors do not prescribe them as often as the two groups above. A person has to take them more than once a day and has to avoid certain foods and drinks when taking them. They, too, may cause side effects, such as sleep problems, dizziness, heart palpitations, and edema (swelling), in some people.

Other drugs used to treat depression are currently not classified into any group. Examples are Effexor (venlafaxine), Wellbutrin (bupropion), Desyrel (trazodone), Serzone (nefazodone), and Remeron (mirtazapine).

In cases of depression with psychosis (loss of touch with reality), the doctor will prescribe antipsychotic medications.

Bipolar Disorders

Like depressive disorders, bipolar disorders affect people's moods, which, in response, affects their actions. But unlike depression, bipolar disorder (sometimes called manic-depressive disorder or illness) is characterized by a down, or depression, followed by an up, or mania. Switching from a manic to depressed state is called cycling. Some people experience rapid cycling, which is defined as more than four episodes a year of either major depression or mania. However, some people switch moods more rapidly than that. The number of episodes varies from person to person and within a particular person over a period of time.

Bipolar disorder that starts in childhood is called childhood-onset bipolar disorder (COBPD). Children with bipolar disorder may have such rapid mood swings that they cycle many times in any given day.

The depression that people with bipolar disorder experience is similar to that suffered by those with depressive disorder. But later they may experience the corresponding mania, which includes a wide range of symptoms.

- Feeling overly confident and doing outrageous things based on this false confidence. For example, saying, and deeply believing, that they are going to be a member of the Olympic track and field team in the upcoming games, which are six months away. They just bought a pair of running shoes and started their training today.

- Sleeping less than usual; in fact, in a state of mania, someone may not sleep all night or for several nights.

- Having racing thoughts. This often results in rapid speech, which may make the person very difficult to understand.

- Being easily distracted. Those who are manic may begin one thing—even one sentence—not finish it, and then start another.

- Following the "pleasure principle" without regard for long-term consequences. For example, people who are manic may go on spending sprees with money they do not have, drive recklessly, use drugs, or engage in promiscuous and unprotected sex.

In her manic state, seventeen-year-old Natalie had decided she wanted to open an art gallery. She emptied her college savings account of all of its $5,000 and maxed out the emergency credit card her parents had given her. She used it to purchase paintings from a street vendor.

A doctor may suspect mania if manic symptoms last for a week or more and begin to affect your schoolwork, home life, and your relationships with other people.

When a manic phase starts, it may feel good or better than good, especially if the feeling comes after a depression. Suddenly you get your school projects done ahead of time, people listen to you talk about your fabulous ideas and plans—at least until they realize that you are being very unrealistic—and you call people and set up social dates. Life is great and so are you.

Because these feelings are so fantastic, people with bipolar disorder often do not want them to go away. They stop seeking treatment, or worse, stop taking their medication. They are willing to live with the consequences because they feel the high is worth the price. They often become addicted to the mania, not unlike people who become addicted to street drugs. And not only do they become addicted to the feelings of euphoria, they also become addicted to the level of productivity they are capable of in this state.

Types of Bipolar Disorder

Bipolar I

Some experts say that bipolar I disorder usually refers to an illness in which a manic attack is followed sometime later by a deep depression. But the episodes do not necessarily "match up." In other words, there is not always a manic episode for every episode of depression. The lengths of time for each episode do not always line up either. For example, a person could be manic for a month and depressed for a year. Bipolar I disorder usually begins in the late teens or early twenties.

Bipolar II

Bipolar II disorder is a mental illness that includes severe depressions (as in bipolar I). However, doctors call the attacks of mania in bipolar II hypomania. The "up" moods of people with this disorder do not go as high. People with hypomania are not really manic and do not do the wild things that people with real mania do. It is important that the doctor do a careful history so that he or she will recognize bipolar II disorder. Antidepressant medication can make the depression turn into mania and cause rapid cycling.

Cyclothymic Disorder

A type of mood disorder with milder mood swings is called cyclothymic disorder, or cyclothymia. Some people who have cyclothymic disorder don't even realize it. Family members and friends say, "Oh, he's just hyper" or "Leave her alone; she's in one of her bad moods."

The mood swings of cyclothymic disorder may be gentle, but they are not harmless. The disorder may keep a person from functioning well in school, jobs, or relationships. Cyclothymia often develops in people between the ages of fifteen and twenty-five.

Experts still have much to learn about cyclothymia. Some say it's a milder, but longer-lasting form of bipolar I disorder. Others say cyclothymia is a condition of its own, but in about half of the people who suffer from it, it eventually turns into bipolar I disorder.

Of course, everyone has mood swings. The less severe, the harder it is to distinguish the disorder from normal moods. There are no physical measurements. Just as it's hard to distinguish the fatigue of a physical illness such as mono (mononucleosis) from everyday tiredness, it is also difficult to distinguish cyclothymia from the normal ups and downs of life.

However, if the mood swings last a long time or go on without significant interruption, the person might decide to see a doctor.

Doctors do have criteria for making a diagnosis. For example, children and teenagers must have had their ups and downs for more than a year with no more than a two-month break.

Treating Bipolar Disorder

Medication

Medication is the most important treatment for bipolar disorder. For more than thirty years, doctors have prescribed one main drug for this condition. Instead of using the trade names Lithonate or Eskalith, people generally use the generic name lithium. Lithium, a salt related to table salt, helps calm a person in the manic phase, evens out a depressed mood, and helps prevent future ups and downs.

People sometimes enjoy their highs. But there are other reasons they may stop taking their lithium. Like almost all medications, lithium can cause side effects, such as an increase in acne, gastrointestinal symptoms (nausea and diarrhea), sleepiness, shakiness, and other coordination problems. "Just the right dose" of lithium is hard to achieve. In other words, the dosage space between what works and what can cause harm to the body is a small one. Therefore, doctors have to monitor the dosage by checking blood levels of the drug. In addition, people sometimes mistake symptoms of too much lithium in their system for a worsening of their manic symptoms or their depression. They say, "This isn't working," and stop taking the medication.

Another group of medications that seems to help the manic phase in some people is the anticonvulsant group (drugs that prevent seizures). One of these is a drug with many names—Depakote or Depakene (sodium valproate, valproate, valproic acid, divalproex sodium). Another is Tegretol (carbamazepine). Not every anticonvulsant works for bipolar disorder, and the anticonvulsants that help some people do not work for others. The side effects of anticonvulsants are usually not serious.

Therapy
If you are a person with bipolar disorder, you may feel tempted to stop taking your medication, especially during a

manic phase. A counselor can help you understand the reasons you need to continue on medication—perhaps for the rest of your life. A therapist can also help you talk about feelings you have about your condition. Therapy, whether one-on-one, group, or family, can help you stay on an even keel.

Besides the various therapies described in the depression section, such as support groups, you will probably need to make some lifestyle changes (such as getting enough sleep and avoiding caffeine, illegal drugs, nicotine, and alcohol). Try to keep stress at manageable levels and don't take on too much.

Mood disorders are complex and hard to cope with. But with education, medication, psychotherapy, and support, you can achieve stability and live a productive life.

Schizophrenia:
A Thought Disorder

Schizophrenia has always been a difficult disease to treat. Even today, there is a great deal of debate concerning what exactly schizophrenia is, what causes it, and how to treat it most effectively. Some facts that mental health professionals do know are:

- Schizophrenia affects 1 in every 100 people in the United States and occurs all over the world.

- The tendency to develop schizophrenia runs in families. It is a hereditary disease.

- There is no single cause of schizophrenia; scientists believe a combination of factors may be responsible.

- Approximately three-fourths of those who have schizophrenia develop it between the ages of sixteen and twenty-five.

- Some of those who subsequently develop schizophrenia had unusual personality traits, such as withdrawal and social isolation, in their younger days.

⮑ Young men tend to develop schizophrenia earlier than young women.

⮑ Schizophrenia usually requires lifelong treatment.

What Is Schizophrenia?

Schizophrenia is primarily a disorder of logical thought. According to the *Diagnostic and Statistical Manual of Mental Disorders* (*DSM-IV*), a doctor should make a diagnosis of schizophrenia only if the following criteria are met.

A. Two or more of the following symptoms have been present during a one-month period:

♦ Delusions

♦ Hallucinations

♦ Disorganized speech

♦ Disorganized or erratic behavior

♦ Catatonic behavior (in which the person remains still for long periods of time)

♦ Symptoms of negative affect, such as a lack of interest in life

Note: Only one of the above symptoms is required if the person has bizarre delusions or auditory hallucinations that involve two voices conversing or one voice constantly commenting on the person's actions.

B. Previous levels of school, work, social, and self-care functions have decreased.

C. The person has had symptoms of the illness for six months or more. This six-month period must include at least one month of symptoms from section A.

D. No other disorder, including bipolar disorder, can account for the symptoms. The symptoms are not caused by a medication, drug, or medical condition.

With these distinct criteria, schizophrenia should be easy to diagnose, but that is not always the case, especially in the early stages of the illness.

Disorders of Thought and/or Behavior

People with schizophrenia have trouble communicating partly because their thoughts are jumbled and don't make sense. For example, people may think their computer is talking to them or that other people can hear what they are thinking. This may be worsened by the fact that many people who suffer from schizophrenia also use illegal drugs.

As a result of these disordered thought processes, those with schizophrenia may develop unusual behaviors that don't make sense to others. For example, people may scratch themselves because they feel that bugs are crawling all over their skin. Or they may say that aliens are telling them to roam the earth, spreading their message of peace.

Hallucinations

Hallucinations are sensory experiences that have no basis in reality. They are created in the minds of the people experiencing them. The most common hallucination is hearing voices. Oftentimes, people with schizophrenia hear voices speaking to them and criticizing. The voices may be those of strangers, friends, family, or famous persons. But no one else can hear the voices. Less frequently people see things that aren't there. Even less often they smell things that no one else smells or taste things that no one else tastes. Hallucinations are frightening—for those who witness their effects and for those having them.

Delusions

As mentioned earlier, delusions are fixed, false beliefs. People hold on to delusions even in the face of reality. People with paranoia may have delusions that people are saying bad things about them or are out to get them.

Disorganized Speech

When in the midst of an episode, the speech of a person with schizophrenia may be as hard to understand as a foreign language. If a person's thoughts are not making sense, the effort to express those thoughts will be very difficult.

Inappropriate Expression of Emotion—Poor Affect

Laughing about a situation that would make anyone else cry, or crying when everyone else is laughing are examples of inappropriate emotional expression. Doctors refer to this as poor or inappropriate affect. Some people show no emotion at all even when faced with extremely sad or exciting situations. In these cases, doctors would say that the person has flat affect.

Lack of Energy and Motivation

An absence of energy and motivation explains why some people with schizophrenia don't take showers or change their clothes very often.

Like those with other mental illnesses, people with schizophrenia experience extremely low moods. They may also have trouble sleeping, be aggressive, or be suicidal.

During the regular appointment with his psychiatrist, Nick, age eighteen, asks the doctor to get him admitted to the hospital. He says he needs help getting back on track. Nick knows he suffers from schizophrenia. "My illness is getting worse," he says. "I'm starting to talk to myself, and the voices are saying weird stuff." Although he says the voices he hears are friendly, he also says he feels depressed and has had strong impulses to hurt himself.

The doctor notes that Nick looks scruffy and unkempt. His long hair is oily and uncombed. He's wearing black denim jeans with holes in the knees, a frayed and faded blue T-shirt, and a dirty white baseball cap.

Nick, who lives with his father, has been hospitalized many times. Most of the times it was because he had forgotten to take his medications. Before his son's last trip to the hospital, Nick's father reported that Nick took off his clothes at the mall, urinated in an outdoor fountain, and barked at the cars in the parking lot.

The doctor is also concerned that Nick has problems with alcohol. Nick says he and his father drink beer together and that he often drinks from five to twelve beers a day.

The first thing Nick's doctor does is make sure that Nick gets the hospital treatment. Then he also insists that Nick's father get help. He encourages them both to enroll in a twelve-step alcohol recovery program. In addition, he helps Nick's father find a therapist who can teach him about his son's disease. Nick's father needs to learn how to take the steps necessary to keep Nick's condition under control, like making sure he takes his medications consistently.

Nick's situation illustrates some of the problems common to many people with schizophrenia. Nick hears voices, feels suicidal, looks messy, and has problems with alcohol. Nick has been in the psychiatric unit before and chances are he will be back again.

The Disease in Between: Schizoaffective Disorder

Schizoaffective disorder combines features of schizophrenia with features of a mood disorder, but it is neither one nor the other. As you may imagine, this disorder is hard to diagnose. Treatment involves combining treatment for schizophrenia with treatment for a mood disorder.

Treatment

If not treated, schizophrenia often gets worse or simply remains unimproved. (Occasionally, there are spontaneous improvements.) Treatment early in the illness can make a great difference. Usually treatment must continue for the long term. Treatment for schizophrenia includes medication, psychotherapy, individual and family education, avoidance of street drugs and alcohol, support groups, and support from family, friends, mental health professionals, and government programs.

Medication

Medication for schizophrenia includes newer drugs with fewer side effects, as well as an older group of medications. They include:

Newer medications	Older medications
Clozaril (clozapine)	Haldol (haloperidol)
Risperdal (risperidone)	Mellaril (thioridzine)
Seroquel (quetiapine)	Navane (thiothixine)
Zyprexa (olanzapine)	Prolixin (fluphenazine)
	Stelazine (trifluoperazine)
	Thorazine (chlorpromazine)
	Trilafon (perphenazine)

Side effects do occur in some people, especially in the early stages of treatment. These include dry mouth, blurred vision, sleepiness or restlessness, and muscle spasms or tremors (shakiness).

Other Treatments and Supports for People with Schizophrenia

Years ago, many people with schizophrenia spent years in mental hospitals. Today, large numbers of those with schizophrenia live successfully in the community. As with most other mental illnesses, medication alone may not be enough to keep symptoms under control. And without support and encouragement, many people stop taking their medications. They may feel like they are better or may hate the side effects. Supportive people can help keep the situation in perspective; the side effects may be bad, but the symptoms of the disease are likely to be worse.

An important, and often neglected, aspect of treatment for people with schizophrenia or other severe mental illness is continuous support. Continuity of care and caregivers is a necessity for those who have communication problems, trouble solving problems, difficulty relating to people, and trouble sorting out their thoughts. Those with schizophrenia need someone that will stick with them and help them with the life tasks that their illness makes difficult to handle. This can be one person, such as a counselor, therapist, or case manager, or it can be an organization.

One such organization in Denver, Colorado, is called the Capitol Hill Action and Recreation Group (CHARG). CHARG Resource Center aims to improve the quality of life and functioning capacity of those with chronic mental illnesses. The organization offers a range of services, including support groups. CHARG is located in a Victorian house with a big yard and a vegetable garden. In addition, there is a drop-in center nearby, an on-site psychiatric clinic, an outreach program for homeless consumers, and advocacy and public education services. There is a recreation and leisure program that offers art groups, team sports, camping trips, and day trips to educational sites. "Many of our people live at the poverty level," says Laurie Sorotkin, director of administrative services. "Because most of them don't own cars, they don't get out of town very often."

Sorotkin and executive director David Burgess, M.S.W., agree that one of the main goals of CHARG is to assist mental health consumers in helping themselves. One way that the organization does this is to employ a partnership, or power-sharing, model. CHARG requires that consumers have a say in the way the organization is run and the services that are offered. Consumers have their own board of directors, which has power equal to that of the other board of directors, the community board. "We believe strongly in this model," says Burgess. "It empowers mental health consumers to manage their own programs, and it works well. The two boards are usually in agreement."

Some mental health consumers have paying jobs at CHARG. Staff member Sorotkin has bipolar disorder. She says that the twenty employed consumers get several benefits: They earn a salary, they get work experience, the job adds structure to their days, and they are involved in CHARG decision-making. Perhaps best of all, they have a sense of community; people help each other.

There are many other community empowerment projects across the country. The Clubhouse Movement, which has more than 200 clubhouses in the United States, provides members with friendship, social activities, housing, educational programs, and vocational programs.

In addition to medication, education about their illness, and consistent care, people with schizophrenia need support. Support groups are helpful, as is the support of family and friends.

Supplemental Security Income (SSI)

As they move toward independent living, those with severe mental illnesses may need financial assistance. Supplemental security income (SSI) helps a person pay for food, housing, clothes, transportation, and entertainment. The person must apply at a local Social Security Administration field office. Because the application is confusing, young people will need help from someone who is familiar with the process. Once a person gets SSI, he or she may be eligible for other government programs, such as vocational rehabilitation (learning a trade), Medicaid (for medical expenses and therapy), food stamps, and housing assistance.

Schizophrenia is a serious mental illness affecting every aspect of a person's life. A combination of medication and other treatment can keep symptoms under control. According to the National Alliance for the Mentally Ill (NAMI), studies show that ten years after treatment, a majority of those with schizophrenia have made some improvement and most can live productive lives.

Self-Help:

What You Can Do

Illnesses are either acute (short-term) or chronic (long-term). Many people live with a chronic illness that tends to flare up when they are under stress. Asthma is a medical condition that allows a person to function normally most of the time, but under stress the person may have an asthma attack.

Mental illness is similar. Many people have periods of wellness punctuated by episodes of symptoms. By keeping track of your symptoms and symptom cycles, you may be able to anticipate and ward off an attack. You will also learn what your stressors are and how to prevent relapses.

Your Symptoms Journal

Keeping a journal of symptoms is an effective way of learning about and understanding your mental illness. Below are suggestions for your symptoms journal.

- Write down any and all symptoms of your mental illness.

- Every night, jot down the date and a short summary of the day, including any stresses that you experienced.

⮑ At the end of every week or two, see if you can find a pattern to your symptoms.

⮑ Bring along your journal to meetings with your doctor or therapist so you can use it to problem-solve together.

Decreasing the Chance of Relapse

A relapse is the return of symptoms after a period of relative freedom from symptoms. Paying attention to your symptoms and why they occur can help you cut down on the severity and frequency of your relapses.

Various factors can cause relapses. Among them are:

⮑ The mental illness itself (cycling) or another physical illness

⮑ Stressful events

⮑ Changes of medications

⮑ Alcohol and drug use

Paying Attention to Warning Signs

We know that mental illnesses come in cycles. When symptoms are minimal, you may believe that your mental illness is cured. But relapses occur, and they are different for each person. You can probably learn to recognize your particular signs of relapse and get help as early as possible, which will decrease the severity of troublesome symptoms.

What to Do

If you believe your mental illness is heading toward a more acute or active phase (a relapse), you might want to do some of the following:

- Get in touch with your doctor, who may decide to try a different type of medication or change the dosage of your current medication.

- Continue with your regular routines, therapy, and support groups.

- Decrease your stress. For example, if you've been going to school and participating in a number of extracurricular activities, you may want to take a break from some of the activities until you feel better.

- Communicate with your family members about how they can help.

- Have a crisis plan ready; carry emergency numbers with you and also post them at home.

The Importance of a Healthy Lifestyle

No matter what your mental illness, you can decrease the chances of relapse with attention to some of the following lifestyle habits.

Eat Well

Mental health advocates advise you to "eat healthy." Try to add more items from the four food groups—fruits, vegetables, grains, and legumes—to your meals and snacks.

Avoid unhealthy foods like chips, soda, candy bars, and fatty meats like bacon.

The following is a list of some healthy foods in each of the four categories that you could choose to add to your diet:

Grains: Include plenty of hot and cold cereals, whole-grain breads, corn, buckwheat, bulgur, and barley in your diet.

Fruits: Citrus fruits, such as oranges, tangerines, and grapefruits, are great. Strawberries and all kinds of melon are also excellent choices.

Vegetables: Raw carrots, celery, cucumbers, broccoli, and cauliflower are all good choices. Use dark green lettuce, such as romaine, in your salads. And don't forget cooked greens, such as collards, kale, mustard, and turnip greens. Also, don't forget to include sweet potatoes, yams, and pumpkin.

Legumes: This category includes beans, peas, and lentils. The group also includes chickpeas (garbanzo beans), refried beans, tofu, tempeh, and soy milk.

If you have a choice between a bowl of ice cream and a bowl of cereal, choose cereal. When you make a sandwich, pile on more lettuce and tomatoes and less meat. Drink plenty of water (eight to ten glasses a day), and avoid high-caffeine drinks like colas and coffee. Try to be mindful of everything that goes into your mouth, and make healthy choices about the food you eat.

Move Your Body

Working out is a great way to improve mental health. Studies show that exercise decreases symptoms of depression.

Most exercise has also been shown to contribute to relaxation, fitness, and the satisfying sense that you've done something good for yourself. Going to a gym or health club may give you access to a swimming pool, free weights, exercise machines, aerobics and cycling classes, and maybe classes in yoga or tai chi.

If a gym is not for you, don't worry. You can get exercise in other ways—with friends or by yourself. Go for a jog in the park. Play fetch with your dog. Ride your bike. Exercise does not have to be painful or leave you gasping for air to be helpful for your mind and your body. Even taking a walk around the block can be enough to help you feel better.

Look Good

How you look on the outside is not a measure of your health or your inner worth. But oftentimes, when you look good, you feel good. Maintaining proper hygiene and wearing clean clothes can do wonders for your mood. Moreover, you may find that when you make an effort to look nice, you receive more positive attention from people around you, which can further contribute to your self-esteem.

Make Time for Fun

Doing something, almost anything, can make you feel better about yourself. Most people have times when they feel like getting out with others; at other times, staying home feels better. The main thing is to listen to your inner urgings to try to figure out what will make you feel better.

Ever since he started school, Raoul has been an outstanding artist. His diagnosis of schizophrenia at age seventeen set him back in many ways. But his heightened sensations add to the eerie quality of his art. Raoul started designing and printing T-shirts, which he sells at bazaars and street fairs.

Not every activity someone suggests will make you happy, but maybe you can find something you would like to do on the following list.

- Listen to music or audiobooks.

- Play a musical instrument.

- Take a walk or a run.

- Do something nice for someone you care about.

- Sketch or paint.

- Meditate, stretch, or do relaxation exercises.

- Clean your room.

- Take a shower or a bath.

Get Enough Sleep

Experts believe that irregular or disrupted sleep cycles can make mental illness worse. That's why it's important to try to get eight hours of shut-eye every night, starting and ending at the same time. Here are some tips to help you get a good night's sleep.

Dos:

- Do exercise every day (but don't do it right before bedtime).

- Do try healthy before-bedtime sleep inducers, such as warm baths, relaxation tapes, reading, warm milk, or a light snack.

- Do try to keep your bedroom at a comfortable temperature—not too hot and not too cold.

- Do take your medication every day.

- Do turn on some soft music or other background noise.

- Do set your alarm and get up when it rings.

Don'ts:

- Don't take sleeping pills or illegal substances to help you sleep.

- Don't drink caffeine-containing drinks (coffee, tea, caffeinated sodas, or hot chocolate) after 3 PM. Better yet, don't drink them at all.

- Don't drink alcohol. Among other things, alcohol can react negatively with your prescribed medications.

- Don't eat heavy, late dinners.

- Don't take naps.

- Don't smoke.

Avoid Alcohol and Street Drugs

"Everybody drinks beer," says Scott. "We have at least one 'kegger' every weekend. My doctor and my parents tell me not to drink and not to smoke. Well, that's a problem for me because my friends already think I'm weird. Besides, those substances help me relax."

Many people, not just those with mental illnesses, use various substances to treat themselves, or to self-medicate.

Substances that people abuse include caffeine, nicotine, alcohol, marijuana, cocaine, inhalants, hallucinogens, narcotics, opiates, stimulants, and sedatives. For people with mental illnesses, using these substances can be dangerous for the following reasons:

- A large percentage of all people who use alcohol or street drugs get addicted to them. If you have a mental illness, you run a great risk of then having two serious problems (a dual diagnosis) to deal with. Researchers say that about half of those with a mental illness also have a substance abuse problem.

- Those with mental illnesses who abuse drugs and alcohol can get into physical trouble because of interactions between these substances and medications.

Doctors who are experts in the dual diagnosis of mental illness and substance abuse recommend special programs that treat both problems at the same time. These programs may be modeled after the twelve-step programs of Alcoholics Anonymous or Narcotics Anonymous, but they also take into consideration the mental illness.

Working on Communication

Even when we try very hard to "do it right," effective communication with the important people in our lives is hard to achieve.

When a mental illness intrudes, effective communication can get even harder than it was before. A person in the acute phase of a mental illness may not be able to work on better communication. But when the acute phase ends, it's time to see what you can do to improve communication with yourself, with family and friends, and with mental health professionals.

Improve Communication with Yourself

We all talk to ourselves. Often what we say to ourselves is negative. Have you ever made statements like "I'm really a no-good person," or "I always make a mess of everything," or "Nobody likes me; I'd be better off dead"? Negative self-talk serves no useful purpose; it only makes us feel terrible. Instead, try affirmations, also called positive self-talk. Make up affirmations that fit you and repeat them over and over to yourself until you believe them.

   ➷ "I try very hard."

   ➷ "I don't like to study, but I'll make myself do it, and later on I'll be happy I did."

☞ "I am getting more mature every day."

☞ "I really am a good person."

Writing regularly in a journal is another way of improving communication with yourself. Your written thoughts may surprise you. Many people find writing is a great way to work through problems. When your frustration or anger is laid out in front of you, it is often much easier to deal with. Expressing yourself can make you feel better. It is also satisfying to have a record of your life for yourself and others.

Improve Communication with Family and Friends
Cultivate friendships. If you have a mental illness, this may be tough. You will have to figure out an answer to the question: How much do I say about my illness? You are the judge.

> Judy's diagnosis is bipolar disorder. She had friends before her diagnosis, and she has made friends since. Judy doesn't hit people over the head with news of her disability. She usually waits until the time seems appropriate. If a new friend reveals something personal, Judy may decide it's time to do the same.

Don't ever feel you have to say anything about yourself that you would rather not say. But promise yourself you will be direct in your communication and ask for what you need. If you're feeling that no one cares about you, there is nothing wrong with saying, "I need a hug today."

Chances are that others are feeling the same way. Your hug will make them feel better, too.

Practice being direct in trying to identify and express your emotions. It's okay to say, "I really feel angry right now. I don't even know why. Maybe I just need some time by myself."

Improve Communication with Professionals and Other Helpers

Remember that when dealing with professionals and other helpers you need to be as direct and honest as you can. Withholding information will not help matters, and it will hold you back from getting the help you need. Also, don't forget to bring your symptoms journal to your doctor visits.

De-Stress/Relax

Stress refers to all of the things that intrude on your life and add to your feelings of being unglued, uptight, or depressed. Examples of things that can cause stress include:

- Trying something, failing at it, and believing you can't try again

- Getting involved in an intimate relationship

- Breaking up an intimate relationship

- Changes in routine

- Illnesses and deaths

- Separations from loved ones

- Too much togetherness with loved ones

Stress is a part of life. There is no way to escape it. The trick is to learn to manage it in healthy ways. Smoking, drinking, using illegal drugs, and having unprotected, promiscuous sex are unhealthy ways in which some people try to cope with stress. Usually these behaviors result in more stress.

Healthy stress relievers include all of the lifestyle changes previously discussed—healthy eating, daily exercise, getting enough sleep, and having fun.

It's also important to find time to relax. Most people have favorite ways of relaxing—watching television, reading the newspaper, listening to music, talking on the phone, sending and receiving e-mail, playing computer games. But if you want to try something new, use one or more of the following techniques.

Be Mindful

Have you ever walked or driven somewhere, arrived at your destination, and then wondered how you got there? Have you ever gone into your bedroom to get something and then wondered what you went in there for?

Being mindful means paying close attention to what you're doing. For instance, you're walking to the bathroom to brush your teeth. As you walk, feel the carpet under your feet, notice the bathroom light. Feel the toothpaste tube as you squeeze it, sniff the minty smell of the toothpaste, watch the paste come out of the tube, listen to the water as it leaves the faucet, feel the brush on your teeth and tongue.

Mindfulness also includes conscious breathing. Being aware of your own breathing is relaxing. Try it. Breathe in; count to five. Breathe out; count to five again. Keep this up for five minutes. Don't you feel more relaxed than when you started?

Mindfulness is a great way to relax because it slows you down and helps you learn to recognize pleasure in simple daily activities. It also helps get your mind off of your troubles.

Meditate

Meditation is the practice of quieting the mind. You may be familiar with the image of people seated, cross-legged, chanting with their eyes closed. This is one way people meditate. At other times, people will focus their eyes on an object in front of them, or just close their eyes and sit quietly. There are many books or group meetings in which you can learn the art of meditation. The basic concept is that you get into a physically comfortable position in a quiet place where you will not be disturbed (turn off your phone, computer, beeper, anything that is likely to distract you or force you to get up) so that you can relax and focus your energy on clearing your mind. Some people clear their mind by keeping their thoughts fixed on an image in front of them. Some concentrate on their breath, while others simply allow their thoughts to flow without giving attention to any particular idea.

Keep in mind that meditation takes practice. When you first try it, you may find that you are fidgety, you keep thinking about the amount of homework you have to do or about the bills you have to pay, and then you criticize yourself for not being able to meditate properly. Relax. As easy as it sounds, meditation is challenging. Some people spend their entire lives perfecting the art of meditation. But you can experience benefits even if you practice just ten or more minutes a day or even every other day. Some people meditate and/or practice other relaxation techniques in the morning before they face the day. Others meditate at bedtime to help them relax. Some practice meditation several times a day. You may find, after consistently practicing for a few weeks or even less, that you're not as anxious or that you're sleeping better (especially if you practice just before bedtime). Not everyone will experience the same results, but one thing is sure, meditation has no negative side effects, and the benefits can only help you.

Use Imagery and Visualization

If depression is part of your mental illness, your brain is probably working overtime on worries and negative scenarios. You will need to retrain your brain to see the world in a more positive light.

Visualization is the mental technique of using your imagination to create pictures in your mind. Have you always wanted to go to Hawaii? Then take a trip there in your mind. Lie on your bed or on the floor. Close your eyes and taste the salt water, let the healing sun soak into your skin, swim with the fish, feel the grains of sand between your toes. Does this procedure sound odd? At least give it a try. You may be amazed by the relaxing and pleasant feelings it brings. And if you find that your imagination isn't up to the task, you can get an audiocassette (such as Emmett E. Miller's *Relaxation and Inspiration* or *Letting Go of Stress*, or Belleruth Naparstek's *Healing Trauma: Guided Imagery and Affirmations*) that will give you step-by-step instructions and help you relax.

Try Progressive Muscle Relaxation

Progressive muscle relaxation involves tensing and then relaxing (one muscle group at a time) as many muscles in your body as you can think of. The best way to do this exercise is to lie on your back on a carpeted floor or a mat.

Start at the top of your body and work down. Begin with your head. Give each muscle group seven seconds of tensing and then let those muscles relax. Using your forehead muscles, make a frown; hold for seven seconds and relax. Scrunch up your nose, relax. Make a kissing motion with your lips. Hold, then relax. Now move to your shoulders. Try to pull both shoulders up to your ears. Relax. Pull your arms close to your sides for seven seconds. Relax. Get the idea? Keep moving down your body until you get to your toes.

This exercise will take ten to fifteen minutes, and you'll feel like a nice, limp dishrag when you get finished.

Swim Standing Up

If you want a relaxation exercise that's a bit more active, pretend you're swimming. You can stand up for this one. Take a breath before swinging your arms backward in a circle as if you're swimming the backstroke. Do this for as many rotations as you can stand. Then reverse directions and circle forward.

Put More Movement into Your Relaxation

If you want regular movement in your meditation, try yoga. Yoga is an ancient practice of combining breathing exercises with physical postures. The word "yoga" means "union"—the union of the body, mind, and spirit. In yoga you will focus your thoughts, quiet your emotions, stretch, and relax. There are many different varieties of yoga that are taught in a growing number of yoga studios and gyms. Some involve more movement while others are focused on meditation techniques and remaining in one position. In order to get familiar with the different practices, you may want to check out a book about yoga or simply start attending classes to find out which type works best for you. Most studios and gyms have beginning classes, which are a great introduction to this discipline.

Get a Massage

A massage for some people is the ultimate in relaxation. There is good news and bad news about massage. The bad news is that a professional massage does not come cheap. Many people can't afford fifty dollars an hour or more for their relaxation. The good news is that you may not need a professional massage. Find a friend who is willing to exchange shoulder rubs. You can start first. Pretend that your friend's shoulder and neck muscles are lumps of bread dough. Squeeze and release. Put a little pressure on the back of his or her head. Work on these tense areas for about ten minutes. Then tell your friend it's his or her turn to act as masseuse.

If you can afford a professional massage, you can get recommendations from friends, recreation centers, health clubs, or schools of massage therapy. Find out if the massage therapists you're considering are certified or if they received their training at a nationally accredited school of massage therapy.

Laugh

Laughter is good medicine; it lifts your mood. When you're depressed, not much seems funny. The important thing is to put yourself in touch with people and situations that might make you laugh. Look for movies and television programs with laugh potential. Read the comics, listen to tapes and CDs that are humorous, or check out all of those forwarded e-mails.

Beware of Negative Thought Patterns

Eliminating negative thoughts is easier said than done. But one thing is certain: You can't get rid of negative thoughts until you realize that you're having them. Below are a few common negative thought patterns.

Catastrophizing

Catastrophizing is the epitome of negative thinking; it means thinking that the absolute worst possible thing that could happen is going to happen. For example: "I've had a bad day, and probably something terrible is going to happen tonight. Tomorrow is likely to be awful, too, just like the rest of my life, so I might as well do away with myself; no one will miss me anyway."

Generalizing

Generalizing is similar to catastrophizing. Those who make negative generalizations come to broad conclusions based on one piece of evidence. For example: "That group of boys was really mean to me. All boys are mean and they all hate me."

Personalizing and Control Issues

Do you assume that whenever anything goes wrong in a situation in which you are involved, it is your fault? Perhaps you and your friends want to go to the movies but when you get there, the movie is sold out. Do you think you are responsible for everyone's disappointment? Or maybe your boyfriend or girlfriend is in a bad mood on your date. Do you immediately think that you're responsible? Unfortunately (or fortunately) the world does not revolve around you, and you do not have absolute control. Believe it or not, many things take place that have nothing to do with you. They are not your responsibility, and you have no control over them.

One of the reasons Cara gets anxious and depressed is because she takes responsibility for everything. She says, "I should never have tried to fix Maggie up with Brad. When they went out last Friday night, they both drank too much, and he crashed his dad's car into a guardrail. Now they're both grounded, and it's all my fault. They're going to hate me."

Mind Reading

Can you read other people's minds? Most of us can't, but some people think they can. Example: "Marcia didn't speak to me this morning. She must hate me."

Emotional Reasoning

Believing that your feelings determine the kind of person you are is an emotional fallacy. Example: "I'm in a crabby mood today; I guess I'm just an angry person."

Being a Perfectionist: "I Should . . ."

Many of us are constantly lamenting the qualities we don't have. We try for perfection. Although it is not bad to strive toward goals, beating yourself up about not being perfect can have some negative consequences. One of the worst is that you never allow yourself to see the great accomplishments you *have* achieved. Perhaps it's time to take a step back and recognize what you have done.

Stopping Negative Thoughts

Thought stopping is a simple process you can practice to get out of the habit of distorted, negative thinking. Whenever you recognize a negative thought, stop it. Replace the negative thought with a positive one.

Negative Thought: I'm such an angry person.
Positive Thought: Sometimes I get angry like everyone else. Anger is a valid emotion. It's what I do with my anger that's important.

Negative Thought: No one likes me.
Positive Thought: I can make a list of several people who like me and who want the best for me.

Negative Thought: I'm worthless.
Positive Thought: No one is worthless. I have tried to do, and have done, many worthwhile things in my life.

Negative thinking is a difficult habit to break. However, with hard work, you can become a more positive-thinking person.

Accepting Your Mental Illness

If you are diagnosed with a mental disorder, you will probably experience a wide range of feelings. You may be relieved that there is finally a name for what has been bothering you. You may feel angry at having to put up with your symptoms while your friends and family lead "normal" lives. Whatever your feelings, it is important to recognize and work through them. Accepting that you have a mental illness can be difficult. You are not like everyone else, but let's face it—nobody is exactly like anyone else. You may have to rely on medication and deal with its potentially unpleasant side effects. You may have to accept that you can't work at any job you choose. The feelings that you experience may be very much like those experienced by those who are grieving a loss. And truly, you are suffering a loss—the loss of the life that you expected to lead.

As with any kind of grief, your feelings of loss will come and go. You may think you are completely over a loss only to have those feelings revived by an event or memory. Some feelings of grief may be with you forever. Grief is a process; the important thing is to let yourself experience it. By understanding these feelings and knowing what to expect, you may find it easier to deal with your illness.

Many years ago, a woman named Elizabeth Kubler-Ross identified five stages people typically experience when they are going through grief. It is important to keep in mind that, though these stages are placed in an order, you may not experience them in this sequence. Also, you may experience one stage, move on to another, and then come back to the first stage again. Each person moves through grief differently and at his or her own pace.

Denial

Denial is often the first stage of dealing with unpleasant news. Denial is the refusal to recognize the pain of loss. Sometimes denial can help you deal with life because it puts off bad feelings until you are prepared to deal with them. But if denial causes you to stop taking necessary medication ("I don't need it; I'm fine without meds"), denial can be extremely harmful.

Anger

Anger is not necessarily a bad emotion. Anger can motivate you to get the help you need. But anger can be destructive when it pushes other people away and leaves you alone. To help defuse your anger, you can use some of the techniques mentioned in this chapter, such as exercise, meditation, thought-stopping, and laughter.

Bargaining

In the bargaining stage, you may try to make a deal— with God, with yourself—with any entity that you hope can make your mental illness disappear. "I'll never yell at my mom again if you just make these voices stop!" Prayer and a strong religious faith help many people with mental illness, but certain problems will remain.

Depression

Once you realize that you're dealing with a mental illness—with your diagnosis and the life changes that come from such a diagnosis—you may feel very down. This grief stage is different from the depression of a mental illness. The depression of a mental illness comes from inside and is unrelated to outside events. The depression of grief will pass as you move on to the final stage of grief: acceptance.

Acceptance

When you get to acceptance, you begin to accept yourself as the unique person you are, a person with a mental illness. You begin to appreciate the good things in your life and welcome each new day.

Value Yourself

Self-esteem, the belief that you are a valuable person, is a difficult feeling for many people to achieve. It is especially hard for those dealing with a mental illness. You did not choose to have a mental illness any more than a person chooses to have pneumonia, diabetes, or seizures. You do, however, have a choice as to what you are going to do about your illness.

Do your affirmations, take your prescribed medications, meet with your therapist and/or your support group, and make lifestyle changes. As a result of doing all of the above, your self-esteem will rise.

What else are you supposed to do to help yourself achieve a feeling of self-worth? Here is a list.

   ➾ Do not compare yourself to other people. You are yourself, unique and wonderful; there is no one else like you.

- Do not put yourself down. Do not say, "I'm so stupid" or "I'm so worthless." Every time you hear yourself making such a remark, stop and silently apologize to yourself. Then resolve not to make such negative statements in the future.

- In any situation, do what you think is right. If what you decided to do turns out wrong, apologize but don't overdo it. You did the best you could.

- Take your prescribed medications and don't use unhealthy means, such as alcohol or illegal drugs, to numb yourself. It's okay and important to feel your emotions, including those that are unpleasant.

- Take any compliments you receive with a simple "thank you." Give sincere compliments to others. Everyone likes to be appreciated.

- Try to surround yourself with others who have high self-esteem. This does not mean you have to hang around with folks who brag all the time. People with high self-esteem do not have to brag. They are secure in themselves.

- Terminate destructive relationships.

It's important to remember that the teen years can be the hardest time of anyone's life. A mental illness will not make matters easier. But with education, awareness, and regard for your own needs, your situation is likely to improve.

Mental health consumer David Coy says, "I attribute my own level of functioning to employment, to medication, and to much psychotherapy. It took many years of experimentation to find a good level and mix of meds that work for me. The benefits of empowerment are many—independence, more money, higher self-esteem, the ability to form relationships outside the human services provider system, freedom to choose housing, transportation, on and on."

If Possible, Get a Job—Or Plan for a Job in the Future

Not everyone with a serious mental illness will be able to hold down a full-time paying job. But almost everyone can find volunteer work for at least a few hours a week or a job with part-time hours. For example, you might be able to volunteer with Habitat for Humanity, building houses for low-income people, or you could offer to read to an elderly person in a nursing home. Or maybe you could handle working at a pet shop two days a week. Working is a great way to build your self-confidence and develop marketable skills.

If you're still in school, your studies may keep you too busy to commit to a job. But it's not too early to think of the future. Work is something to think about and plan on doing.

Filling out job applications can be confusing. Ask your parents or social worker for help. Here are some job application and interview suggestions:

⮞ Try to fill out applications ahead of time or take them home with you and bring them back the next day.

- Tell the truth. Lying on a job application could get you in trouble.

- Although you are not going to lie, you also do not have to go into great detail about your mental health history. Try to think ahead of time about what you're going to say.

- Dress for success. Get advice from family and friends about what looks appropriate for a job interview.

- Find people who are willing to be references for you and let them know that someone will contact them.

- Throughout the process be cheerful and positive.

David Coy is not a teenager anymore, and his philosophy has evolved over many years. He says, "Work has always been my salvation from mental illness. I function much better when I have a job to go to, no matter how menial. I need a reason to get out of bed each day and a place to go. Losing myself in work and establishing relationships with coworkers does more for me than all of the psychotherapy that money can buy."

Your Rights

The Americans with Disabilities Act (ADA) stands behind you in your efforts to find meaningful employment. According to the ADA, businesses that have fifteen or more employees cannot discriminate against a qualified worker because of a mental illness. The workplace must also make special arrangements, such as flexible schedules, for those with disabilities.

Set Realistic Goals

Above all, set realistic goals. Having a job may not be a realistic goal for you right now. Staying in school may be. Some people with mental illnesses have unrealistic ideas and goals they can't reach. Then, when they don't reach those goals, they feel like failures.

Recovery from mental illness will not happen overnight. But there is much you can do to help yourself.

Suicide Prevention

Andy did not try to commit suicide, but he remembers considering it after his parents took the car keys away from him. Recently they had gotten on his nerves big time; this was the last straw. He remembers thinking, I'll teach them. They'll be sorry when I'm gone. Andy's thinking was partly right. His parents would have been more than sorry; they would have been overwhelmed with sorrow and guilt. Andy realized in time that he wouldn't have been around to enjoy their tears.

Parents, siblings, and friends of a person who commits suicide suffer from almost unbearable guilt. What did they do wrong? What might they have done to prevent this?

Suicide Prevention—For You

According to a recent national study, suicide is the third leading cause of death among young people between the ages of fifteen and nineteen. This figure represents a rate that has tripled since 1960. In her book, *Night Falls Fast: Understanding Suicide,* Kay R. Jamison says that every seventeen minutes someone in America commits suicide.

All of the major mental illnesses bring with them the threat or risk of suicide. But many more people consider the idea than actually go through with it. Even people who think about suicide don't think about it all the time. When you are not thinking about suicide is the time to put some prevention plans in place.

Undoubtedly the worst thing about suicide is its finality. That's the part young people don't really understand. Actors who die in movies come back to star in the next one. But even older people have suicide fantasies such as "They'll miss me when I'm gone," as if they'll be around to see.

If you are a person who has thought of suicide, or if you're afraid you might consider it sometime in the future, try some of these tips before you get to the edge.

→ Make a supreme effort to stick to your lifestyle changes—eat and sleep as well as you can, keep taking your prescribed medications and communicating with your therapist, attend a support group and interact with other people, use positive-thinking and relaxation techniques, and build some fun into your day.

➷ If you slip up on some of the above, don't beat yourself up. So you eat a pile of greasy fries three days in a row. It's not the end of the world.

➷ Set achievable goals.

➷ Give more weight to your successes than to your "failures." Kenny not only got up at 8 AM, he also ate breakfast and fed the dog. "Good for me," he said to himself. He gave himself a pat on the back and his dog a pat on the head.

➷ If you don't already have a bulletin board in your bedroom, get one. Decorate it with pictures of friends and family, uplifting messages and verses, souvenirs of happy trips and events, and reminders of happy times to come.

➷ Write in your journal. Record your thoughts and feelings. If you like to draw, include some pictures.

If you believe you are in immediate danger of suicide, consider the following:

➷ Don't let yourself be alone.

➷ Talk to as many supportive people for as long as you can talk and for as long as they will listen. If you tire one person out, find someone else who will listen. Express you emotions. Get it all out. Talking is very helpful.

↪ Get rid of any and all possible means of suicide. Let someone else hold on to your medications, don't let anyone keep guns in your house, and don't even think of hanging out with someone who might have a gun.

↪ Call your doctor when you're feeling more depressed than usual or at the first thought of suicide. (Some people who are feeling actively suicidal get themselves checked into a hospital until they feel better.)

Taking these actions does not mean you're weird; it means you're smart. And even if you think you've tried everything, remember that you do have options. Suicide is never the only option. There are always more things to try. Maybe you haven't given yourself enough time to see results. Maybe you haven't tried the right combination of medications and other treatments. Have courage. Keep reaching for the glimmer of hope.

If Someone You Love
Has a Mental Illness

Supportive friends and relatives can make a positive difference in the lives of those with a mental illness. They want to help. But how?

> Pete is now grown and has two kids of his own. His mental illness was not correctly diagnosed until he turned thirty. Recently his mother asked, "When you were a teenager, what would have helped?"
> "I don't know," Pete said. "What did you do?"
> "Well, we took you to a therapist."
> "And I didn't want to go. I already felt different from my friends." Pete shook his head. "The main thing is that you worried about me. You put up with me, and you didn't give up. Now I can appreciate that."

Cultivate Patience and Understanding

The most important qualities for the "helper" are patience, understanding, and being there for the long haul. Can you understand what's going on inside the head of someone in a manic phase of bipolar disorder or someone with schizophrenia? You can't, but you can try. Imagine yourself watching a movie in which the characters are speaking three different languages at once or the subtitles are whizzing backward and upside down across the screen.

How does it feel to have schizophrenia?

Imagine yourself in a carnival fun house. The mirrors distort your body, the colors are psychedelic, the loud noise gives you a headache, and you can't figure out who's talking. Imagine now that there is no way out of this place.

How does it feel to have a bipolar condition?

Imagine yourself so wired that you can't sleep for three nights in a row, you can't stop talking even when people tell you you're not making sense. You ran up a $2,000 bill on your parents' credit card, and you've just crashed their car. Someone tells you that you're acting manic. But you feel great. Why should you be concerned?

Imagine that your major relief from these moods and sensations comes from medicine that makes your mouth dry, gives you diarrhea, makes your vision blurry, or causes you to gain weight.

You may find the actions of those with a mental illness disturbing but so do those who *have* the mental illness. Would you like to be feared, shunned, or laughed at? Once you start empathizing, it may become easier to deal with your loved one who is mentally ill.

Be a Friend

To have a friend is to be a friend. That old saying will be especially true in your relationship with the person who has a mental illness.

⇒ Treat your friend or relative with respect.

⇒ Keep your attitude as positive as you can.

➷ Don't take aggressive remarks or actions personally.

➷ Make requests in a clear and direct way.

Recognize and Accept Your Feelings

If someone in your family has a mental illness, you will have to sort out your own feelings about the illness. The best thing you can do for yourself and for the person you love (and maybe, at times, hate) is to recognize that these feelings are normal.

Why Me?

You may wonder why you're the one of all your friends who has a sibling with a mental illness. Why couldn't the illness be something like appendicitis that surgery can cure, or something like asthma that isn't embarrassing?

Sierra talks about her older sister Courtney who is eighteen. "A few years ago my parents took us both to a psychiatrist. We had nearly killed each other several times. Life in our family was horrible, and our parents were scared. I think we all felt crazy. The therapist diagnosed Courtney with bipolar disorder. It was a relief in a way. For example, it explained why she came into my room and turned my dresser drawers upside down when she couldn't find her hairbrush. I never invite my friends over when she's there, and she has already cost me one boyfriend. Sometimes I wonder how I got a sister like her. On the other hand, she's the one who got the mental illness. She didn't ask to have it."

Why Not Me?

Your feelings may include guilt. Why did my sister or brother get the mental illness instead of me? Your feelings may also include fear. If mental illness runs in families, am I going to get it? Your feelings might include a confusing kind of envy. Why does he or she get all the attention in this family?

What can you do with your feelings? First, accept them. Don't try to bury them. Express them in a nonhurtful way. If you don't acknowledge your feelings and if you don't bring them out into the open, you may "explode" at the wrong time or end up abusing drugs or alcohol to dull your pain. Some of the best things you can do are:

⮎ Talk to an understanding friend, someone you trust.

⮎ Get a therapist or a counselor of your own to talk to.

⮎ Find a support group for parents or siblings of young people who have chronic conditions.

⮎ Express your feelings in family therapy sessions.

⮎ Accept the fact that you are not perfect; forgive yourself for your mistakes.

⮎ Realize that your loved one is going through similar grieving.

Take Care of Yourself

As a friend or family member of a person with a mental illness, you have to take care of yourself. Taking care of

109

yourself sets an example of self-care for the person you're trying to help. You need to practice many of the same self-help strategies you recommend to your friend or family member. You need to eat well, get enough sleep, exercise as often as possible, and find support. Imagine what will happen to your loved one if you fall apart. You need to schedule time for yourself. Devoting all of your free time to the person with a mental illness will not do either of you much good.

Be an Advocate for the Mentally Ill

Advocating is simply the act of publicly showing your support for a cause, group, or individual. You can be an advocate for people with a mental illness by supporting the political and social organizations that work for equal rights or that educate the public about mental illness. For example, you can join NAMI (the National Alliance for the Mentally Ill). For ways to contact this and other similar organizations, see Where to Go for Help at the end of this book.

As a member of such organizations, you will be helping to:

⮥ Decrease the stigma and discrimination against people with mental illnesses

⮥ Call attention to the need for more research into the causes of mental illnesses and ways to control them

⮥ Provide more resources and programs for those with mental illnesses

You can also do your part to stamp out myths and misconceptions about mental illness. The following are other actions you may choose to take:

- Help people to understand that mental illnesses are very common. More than six million Americans have some kind of mental illness.

- Teach people that medical science is working to learn more about prevention, causes, and possible cures for mental illnesses.

- Help people to understand that people do not bring mental illnesses upon themselves. Mental illness has a strong biologic basis and mental illnesses are not contagious.

Jane is an advocate for Gus, who lives on her block and has schizophrenia. "His parents bought the house for him," says Jane. "He likes to come by and talk with me when I'm out in the yard. He's such a nice young man. But when he doesn't take his medication, he chases cars. A while back, some of the neighbors got up a petition to try to get him to move. Was he hurting them? No. I joked with them and said that they were the crazy ones. We ended up having a logical discussion about human rights and the petition got dropped."

What to Tell Other People

When considering what to say about your friend or loved one's mental illness, it's a good idea to prepare several explanations, one for intimate friends and close family members, another for casual acquaintances. Keep in mind that you do not owe anyone an explanation. Besides, you need to consider the importance of confidentiality. If the tables were turned and you were the person with a mental illness, would you want someone to tell the whole world about your diagnosis?

To close friends, use this question as your guide: Will this person be sympathetic and give us support? If the answer is yes, you can choose which details you want to tell. For those who are just curious, keep the story simple. You might say that your friend or relative has a chemical imbalance that affects his or her behavior. Or you can choose to politely let those people know you don't wish to discuss the subject with them.

What to Do If Someone You Love Has a Dual Diagnosis

Studies show that half of those with a mental illness also have substance abuse problems. It's obvious that if someone you love has problems with alcohol or street drugs in addition to a mental illness, that person has two problems. In spite of their insistence that they can do it themselves, few people can deal with a substance abuse problem on their own. You can at least try to confront the denial. But at the same time, realize that their acceptance of both their problems may take a long time.

NAMI offers these additional suggestions:

⇔ Do not think of the addiction as a family disgrace.

~ Do believe that recovery from addiction is possible.

~ Try not to nag, preach, or lecture about the addiction. The person has heard that already.

~ Do not let the person talk you into drinking or using with him or her.

~ Do not expect an immediate recovery or a 100 percent recovery. Most people have relapses.

~ Try to get help for both conditions at the same time.

~ Think of ways to encourage and motivate the person, but understand that you can't do it for them.

~ Continue to offer your love and emotional support.

What to Do If Things Get Scary: Handling Anger, Hallucinations, Delusions, and Violent Behavior

Hallucinations or Delusions

Remember that what seems ridiculous to you is real to the person with a mental illness. Trying to talk people out of something they perceive to be real is an exercise in futility. A better strategy is to tune in to the emotion, such as fear. Let the person know that you will do whatever you can to help that person feel safe. Also, it's important for you to take whatever measures you need to feel safe yourself.

Handling Anger

When faced with another person's anger, most of us have a tendency to get angry ourselves. Your anger will only escalate the situation. When faced with the anger of a friend or relative who has a mental illness, keep in mind the following tips:

- Try to figure out if the anger comes from a rational (reasonable) or irrational cause.

- Acknowledge the anger and tell the person that you are trying to understand the reasons for it.

- Do not argue back.

- Stay calm and give the appearance of being in control.

- Give the person a chance to calm down and to back down.

- If necessary, call for help.

What to Do If Someone You Love Is Accused of a Crime

If your family member with a mental illness is accused of a crime, get a lawyer. Do not allow the police to question the person who has a mental illness without a lawyer present. If you can't afford a lawyer or don't have any idea where to find one, call your local bar association or public defender's office. Keep calm. If you ask for a lawyer, the police must stop questioning the person. If the police pick up a person with a mental illness, it does not mean that the police will arrest the person.

The National Alliance for the Mentally Ill offers a free fact sheet, "Dealing with the Criminal Justice System," as well as "A Guide to Mental Illness and the Criminal Justice System," which is available for five dollars. Call 1-888-780-4167 and ask for Number R407.

What to Do If Someone You Love Talks About Suicide

When things seem to be spinning out of control, a person may think about suicide, talk about it, and even try to do it. If you suspect that someone you care about is considering suicide, trust your instincts and do something. The most important thing you can do for your loved one is to be aware. Here are some cues to watch and listen for. A person may be suicidal if he or she:

- Talks a lot about death or is preoccupied by someone else's suicide

- Repeatedly talks around the subject of suicide or makes statements such as "The world would be better without me in it" or "I'd be better off dead"

- Withdraws from friends or fights a great deal with them and stops doing fun things

- Starts neglecting his or her appearance

- Begins to heavily abuse alcohol or street drugs

- Stops going to school

⮑ Takes unnecessary risks, such as driving too fast

⮑ Gives away personal possessions or stops talking about the future

What You Can Do
The most important thing you can do for someone who believes he or she has run out of options is to take that person seriously.

Don'ts

⮑ Don't ignore even the hint of a threat.

⮑ Don't try to be a substitute therapist. Call upon a professional.

⮑ Don't worry that talk of suicide is going to make the person do it.

Dos

⮑ Do listen carefully and find out as much as you can about what the person is thinking and feeling.

⮑ Do let the person know you care about his or her feelings and that you will do whatever you can to help.

⮑ Do give the person reasons for hope.

⮑ Do explore resources. Both of you might want to carry with you a list of resources, including the phone numbers of the person's therapist, trusted adults, such as a teacher or school counselor, a suicide prevention hotline, or the police department.

⤳ Ask the person who mentions suicide if he or she has a plan for suicide. If a plan such as a gun or pills exists, do not leave the person alone. Get help.

A Few Coping Ideas from Those Who Have "Been There"

"Put agreements in writing. That way you'll avoid arguments about who said what and when."

"Give the person space—physical and emotional."

"Don't do things for people that they can do for themselves."

"Even though you're not in their face every minute, let them know you're there for them."

"Don't consider people stupid just because they have a mental illness. Don't talk down to them."

"Get outside with your relative or friend. Walking and talking go well together."

"Give the person with a mental illness credit for all he has accomplished in spite of the illness."

At times you may feel helpless and hopeless, but don't underestimate your importance. Your friend or loved one needs you.

Hope for the Future

There is hope for the future for those with mental illness. Hope includes discoveries about the causes of mental illness. Hope includes new treatments. Hope includes better understanding and acceptance of mental illness. Finally, hope comes from the many individuals with mental illness who are living productive lives. Below are the true stories of three such people.

Mark's Story

Several years ago Mark was a different person from the guy he is now. Back then he might not have believed his story belonged with the stories of others who are "making it." Now he does.

Mark says that when he was a kid, he had no clue that mental illness would hit him of all people. "Except I know now that my grandfather had schizophrenia and my mother was manic depressive."

He thinks his mental illness began when he was sixteen. When he was fifteen, his younger brother died. After that, Mark's depression went on for so long, his friends started getting worried about him.

Mark says, "The psychiatrist I saw at University Hospital couldn't decide if I had bipolar disorder or schizophrenia.

I know it's hard to tell sometimes. Maybe he flipped a coin. Anyway, he put me on medication for bipolar disorder. Two years ago another doctor evaluated me and said I had schizoaffective disorder, which is sort of a cross between the two."

Although Mark believes strongly in the value of medication and takes his medication regularly, he says, "Over the years I've felt sort of like a guinea pig. You name it—I've had it. My side effects were the worst on Haldol. My muscles got so stiff, I had to go into the hospital for a week to get weaned off of it."

Mark talks freely about his mental illness but sees no need to confide in the people he works with. "I work at a regular job," he says, "and there's still a stigma to mental illness. They don't need to know."

Although Mark, twenty-six, has a support system, he has also done a lot for himself. He spent his teen years in a group home, finishing high school while he lived there. Mark is proud of his accomplishments—he holds down a part-time job at a warehouse, he lives in his own apartment, and he cleans and cooks for himself. His therapist recently got him involved in an outdoor program, which will allow him to go skiing, backpacking, and camping. Mark gets some money from SSI, which he supplements by working. He says his biggest help was the housing, which he obtained with the help of Servicios de la Raza, a mental health and social services center and community service organization. Mark pays a percentage of his income for rent.

He gives the following advice to young people who get a diagnosis of mental illness. "First," he says, "accept it.

You can't get away from it. The mental illness may stay with you for the rest of your life. Also," he adds, "learn to accept your limitations. I used to try to work sixty-four hours a week. Now I work part-time. I have an understanding boss, who lets me vary my hours according to how I'm feeling. Second, take your meds. And third, keep busy. Keep your mind occupied so you don't focus on your illness. Work, go to school, do whatever."

Mark agrees that support, wherever you can find it, is important. Part of his support comes from the family of his adopted half-sister. He used to go to a support group for young people with various kinds of chronic illnesses, but he doesn't need that right now. "Sure, I have a mental illness," he says, "and I accept that, but most of the people I meet don't even know about it."

Sam's Story

She doesn't give a specific diagnosis, but she has a mental illness, and she's willing to talk about it. She's willing to talk even more if she knows her real name will not appear in a book. "Call me Sam," she says.

Sam shares some information about herself and what she has accomplished in spite of her mental illness. Or, what she has accomplished because of it. Samantha grew up in Kansas and got her bachelor's degree from the University of Kansas. She wanted to be a social worker, so she got her graduate degree (M.S.W.) in social work at the University of Missouri. Later, Sam got another college degree—this time in creative writing. "I try to make sense of my mental illness, using these skills," she says.

Samantha worked for a time in a nursing home. Although she found the job stressful, she realized she liked working with people. "Since that time," she says, "I've always tried to do some work with people contact. It's mandatory for my development."

Sam believes strongly in medication. "My mental illness was misdiagnosed for fifteen years. Turns out I was taking the wrong medication, but I stayed on it because it helped!" Samantha says one of the side effects of medication is that she gained weight. But she believes the benefits outweigh any potential inconvenience or discomfort. Samantha also has a great deal of respect for psychiatrists. "It's got to be a hard job," she says. "Each individual has a different body chemistry from everyone else, so it's sort of hit or miss with medications. The doctors have to try a lot of different ones. And they don't always see instant results." She believes that anyone who has ever been psychotic will do whatever it takes to avoid that state. "You remember it, you feel ashamed, and it leads to low self-esteem."

Samantha doesn't rely entirely on medication to help her through the hard times. She faithfully attends a twelve-step program, Emotions Anonymous. The group she attends meets weekly on Mondays from 7:30 to 9 PM.

In the future, Samantha, who has written several books for children, is looking forward to illustrating them. Although the tendency to mental illness appears to be inherited, so does her artistic talent. "My mother was a freelance artist," Sam says with pride. "She was able to raise eight kids as a single parent."

David's Story

David Coy of Meadville, Pennsylvania, is a consumer of mental health services and has served as a member of his county's human services board, as well as its president. The following excerpts are from one of David's talks.

He says, "I have a genetic chemical imbalance in my brain, namely 'bipolar affective disorder,' or in layman's terms, 'manic-depressive.' This condition appears to have been inherited from the maternal side of my family. Numerous cousins, aunts, and uncles have suffered from and been treated for this disorder. Of my mother's five children, four of us have undergone treatment in mental hospitals. I myself was not correctly diagnosed until I was close to thirty years old.

"I have, while in the usually brief manic phase of my illness (typically three or four weeks), been extremely psychotically delusional, believing, for instance, that I was in a movie being filmed by hidden cameras and that everyone I encountered was a paid actor. I have believed radio and television were directly speaking only to me. Once on a California beach I believed I could control the tides and waves of the ocean because the off-shore oil rigs were actually vast pumps under my direction.

"Then, during the long agonizing depressive phase of my illness (sometimes lasting as long as a year or more), I thought constantly of suicide, spent all of my time in bed never caring about housework or even changing the sheets. I didn't take care of myself at all.

"I have had some run-ins with the police as well, while acting out my psychosis, although I've never been convicted of any crime more serious than hitchhiking on the freeway. Once I spent eleven days in a glass cage in a jail of a large city.

"I was not treated for mental illness until age nineteen after a suicide attempt. (I spent three days in a coma with grand mal seizures from overdosing on three bottles of over-the-counter sleeping pills.)

"Since age nineteen I have had around twenty hospitalizations, the shortest three days, the longest a year, a month, and fourteen days in a huge state hospital in California.

"The responsible members of my family have been extremely supportive in recent years, but in our neighborhood when I was nineteen, the stigma of being a mental patient was considered to be an indelible stain upon a person's character, and so my family's response to my suicide attempt was to keep me at home, hidden away. I spent my days and nights in pajamas watching television and sleeping a great deal. A minister of a Unitarian church I had attended gave me some inexpert counseling, but he was wise enough to realize his lack of training in working with the seriously mentally ill and he understood that I was at high risk of re-attempting suicide. He called my family and insisted that I see a psychiatrist. When told to mind his own business, he called the police. The police explained that my family could be held liable if I died, and so, since there was no psychiatrist in Crawford County at that time, I was taken to Oil City and given six electroshock treatments. Although much was erased from my memory, the depression lifted. As soon as I was well enough, I bolted. For four years I was one of the homeless mentally ill.

"I remember a story I heard about a man who was driving past a mental hospital when he had a flat tire. While changing it, he somehow bumped into the lug nuts and they disappeared down a grate. A patient from the hospital who was watching through the fence suggested that the man take one nut from each of the remaining three wheels and place them on the spare, which would get him to a garage to replace the missing ones. 'Wow! That's really smart! I thought you were supposed to be crazy.' 'Well,' replied the patient, 'I may be crazy but that doesn't make me stupid.'

"Recovery means different things to different people, but of all of the many thousands of consumers I have encountered, I do not believe that there is a single one, including myself, who cannot improve his or her level of functioning. It takes hard work, it takes many setbacks, and it takes courage. But the striving should never cease."

Glossary

affect How inner feelings are shown externally, such as by posture or facial expression.

antianxiety agents Medications that depress the activity of the central nervous system and relieve uneasy feelings.

antidepressants A group of medications used to lift low moods.

antipsychotics A group of medications used to treat psychosis, or a person's lack of being in touch with reality.

anxiety disorders Conditions that have anxiety as the primary disruptive symptom.

behavioral therapy A type of counseling that aims to change negative behaviors.

biopsychosocial model of mental illness A way of looking at mental illness that takes into consideration the interrelated aspects of a person's life, including the biological, psychological, and social.

bipolar disorder A severe mental illness that includes episodes of mania and depression.

catatonic A state sometimes seen in those with schizophrenia in which the person remains in a fixed, unresponsive position for a long period of time.

cognitions The mental processes of thinking, knowing, learning, judging, and understanding.

cognitive therapy Counseling based on changing a person's destructive or unhealthy thought patterns.

compulsions Repetitive behavior a person does in response to obsessive thoughts.

confidentiality The agreement between a person and the therapist that whatever the person says will not be revealed to anyone else without permission, except in certain circumstances.

cyclothymic disorder A mild form of bipolar illness in which the mood swings are less severe.

day treatment programs Mental health treatment that allows the person involved to go home at night.

depression A mood disturbance characterized by a lack of interest in formerly pleasurable activities, sadness, discouragement, tiredness, insomnia, helplessness, hopelessness, and worthlessness.

dysthymia Low-grade depression.

electroconvulsive therapy (ECT) A severe but fast-acting treatment for depression that sends a low voltage electrical signal through the brain.

episode A period of mental illness flare-up.

genetic Pertaining to the genes and their influence on the mind and body.

group therapy A type of counseling that facilitates change as a result of interactions among group members.

hallucinations Sensory experiences not caused by external events.

manic phase Episode of bipolar disorder in which the person feels unusually happy or high.

mental status examination Diagnostic testing of a person's emotional, psychological, intellectual, and personality functioning.

mood disorder A condition that affects a person's feelings and ways of relating to the world.

mood stabilizers Medications that help keep a person's emotions on an even keel.

obsessions Persistent thoughts that the mind cannot seem to get rid of.

obsessive-compulsive disorder (OCD)   A mental disorder in which the person performs various rituals in response to repetitive thoughts.

panic attacks   Episodes of unpredictable and acute anxiety in which the person feels fear or terror and has accompanying shakiness, dizziness, sweating, and/or chest pains.

paranoia   The unfounded feeling some people have that everyone is talking about them or is out to get them.

psychosis   Inability to distinguish between internal and external reality; being out of touch with reality.

psychotherapy   Various approaches to treatment of mental disorders in which the person and the therapist talk about feelings, problems, and life experiences as a way of alleviating symptoms and developing better coping skills.

rapid cycling   A condition that exists when a person has more than four episodes in one year of either major depression or mania.

relapse   The return of symptoms after a symptom-free period.

relaxation techniques   Deep breathing and other treatments that help the person relax by concentrating on pleasant, stress-free sensations.

residential treatment center   A twenty-four-hour, inpatient treatment facility for those with mental disturbances.

schizophrenia   A severe mental disorder characterized by disorganized thoughts, speech, and behavior, as well as delusions and hallucinations.

seasonal affective disorder (SAD)   A type of depressive illness in which people feel sad in winter and normal or unusually happy in summer.

seizure   A sudden change in consciousness accompanied by severe electrical discharge of the brain.

Where to Go for Help

In the United States

American Academy of Child & Adolescent Psychiatry
3615 Wisconsin Avenue NW
Washington, DC 20016-3007
(202) 966-7300
Web site: http://www.aacap.org

American Association of Suicidology
4201 Connecticut Avenue, NW Suite 408
Washington, DC 20008
(202) 237-2280
Web site: http://www.suicidology.org

American Foundation for Suicide Prevention
120 Wall Street, 22nd Floor
New York, NY 10005
(888) 333-AFSP (2377)
(212) 363-3500
Web site: http://www.afsp.org

American Psychological Association
750 First Street NE
Washington, DC 20002-4242
(800) 374-2721
Web site: http://www.apa.org

The Center for Mental Health Services (CMHS)
Knowledge Exchange Network (KEN)
P.O. Box 42490
Washington, DC 20015
(800) 789-2647
Web site: http://www.mentalhealth.org

The Child and Adolescent Bipolar Foundation
1187 Wilmette Avenue, P.M.B. #331
Wilmette, IL 60091
(847) 256-8525
Web site: http://www.bpkids.org

Federation of Families for Children's Mental Health
1101 King Street, Suite 420
Alexandria, VA 22314
(703) 684-7710
Web site: http://www.ffcmh.org

Mental Illness Education Project (*The Bonnie Tapes*)
P.O. Box 470813
Brookline Village, MA 02447
(617) 562-1111
Web site: http://miepvideos.org/index.html

National Alliance for the Mentally Ill (NAMI)
Colonial Place Three
2107 Wilson Boulevard, Suite 300
Arlington, VA 22201-3042
(800) 950-NAMI (6264)
(703) 524-7600
Web site: http://www.nami.org

National Foundation for Depressive Illness
P.O. Box 2257
New York, NY 10116
(800) 239-1265
Web site: http://www.depression.org

The National Information Center for Children and Youth
  with Disabilities
P.O. Box 1492
Washington, DC 20013-1492
(800) 695-0285
Web site: http://www.nichcy.org

National Institute of Mental Health (NIMH)
NIMH Public Inquiries
6001 Executive Boulevard, Room 8184, MSC 9663
Bethesda, MD 20892-9663
(800) 421-4211
Web site: http://www.nimh.nih.gov

National Mental Health Association
1021 Prince Street
Alexandria, VA 22314-2971
(800) 969-NMHA (6642)
Web site: http://www.nmha.org

National Mental Health Consumers' Self-Help Clearinghouse
1211 Chestnut Street, Suite 1207
Philadelphia, PA 19107
(800) 553-4KEY (4539)
Web site: http://www.mhselfhelp.org

Suicide Awareness\Voices of Education (SA\VE)
P.O. Box 24507

Minneapolis, MN 55424-0507
(612) 946-7998
Web site: http://www.save.org

Suicide Prevention Advocacy Network (SPAN)
5034 Odin's Way
Marietta, GA 30068
(888) 649-1366
Web site: http://spanusa.org

Yellow Ribbon Suicide Prevention Program
P.O. Box 644
Westminster, CO 80030
(303) 429-3530
Web site: http://www.yellowribbon.org

In Canada

American Foundation for Suicide Prevention
Halifax Chapter
1557 Hollis Street, Suite 634
Halifax, NS B3J 3V4
(902) 426-4959
Web site: http://www.afsp.org

Canadian Mental Health Association
2160 Yonge Street, 3rd Floor
Toronto, ON M4S 2Z3
(416) 484-7750
Web site: http://www.cmha.ca

Mood Disorders Association of British Columbia
2730 Commercial Drive, #201
Vancouver, BC V5N 5P4

(604) 873-0103
Web site: http://www.lynx.net/~mda/

Schizophrenia Society of Canada
75 The Donway West, Suite 814
Don Mills, ON M3C 2E9
(800) 809-HOPE (4673)
Web site: http://www.schizophrenia.ca

Web Sites

Dealing with Depression
http://www.depression-info.com

Health Touch
http://www.healthtouch.com

Pendulum Resources—Bipolar Disorders Portal
http://www.pendulum.org

Schizophrenia Support Organizations
http://members.aol.com/leonardjk/support.htm

Whispers of Sadness (Dysthymic Disorder Support Network)
http://members.tripod.com/whispers_of_sadness

For Further Reading

Carter, Rosalynn. *Helping Someone with Mental Illness.* New
    York: Times Books, 1998.
Crook, Marion. *Suicide: Teens Talk to Teens.* Bellingham, WA:
    Self-Counsel Press, 1997.
Duke, Patty, and Gloria Hochman. *A Brilliant Madness.* New
    York: Bantam Books, 1993.
Fassler, David, M.D., and Lynne Dumas. *Help Me, I'm Sad:
    Recognizing, Treating, and Preventing Childhood and
    Adolescent Depression.* New York: Viking Penguin, 1998.
Gilbert, Paul. *Overcoming Depression.* New York: Oxford
    University Press, 1998.
Gorman, Jack M. *Essential Guide to Psychiatric Drugs, 3rd ed.*
    Upland, PA: DIANE Publishing Co., 1997.
————. *The New Psychiatry: The Essential Guide to State-
    of-the-Art Therapy, Medication, and Emotional Health.*
    New York: St. Martin's Press, 1996.
Hatfield, Agnes B., and Harriet P. Lefley. *Surviving Mental
    Illness: Stress, Coping and Adaptation.* New York:
    Guilford Publications, Inc., 1993.
Helfgott, Margaret, and Tom Gross. *Out of Tune: David
    Helfgott and the Myth of Shine.* New York: Warner Books,
    Inc., 1999.
Hyde, Margaret O., and Elizabeth Forsyth, M.D. *Know
    About Mental Illness.* New York: Walker Publishing
    Company, 1996.
Jamison, Kay Redfield. *Touched with Fire: Manic-Depressive
    Illness and the Artistic Temperament.* New York: The Free
    Press, 1994.

————. *An Unquiet Mind: A Memoir of Moods and Madness.* New York: Random House, Inc., 1995.

Kim, Henry H. *Depression.* San Diego, CA: Greenhaven Press, Inc., 1999.

Klebanoff, Susan. *Ups & Downs: How to Beat the Blues and Teen Depression.* New York: Price, Stern, Sloan, 1998.

Lewis, Cynthia Copeland. *Teen Suicide: Too Young to Die.* Springfield, NJ: Enslow Publishers, Inc., 1994.

Mondimore, Francis M. *Depression, the Mood Disease.* Baltimore: Johns Hopkins University Press, 1995.

Perry, Angela, M.D., ed. *The AMA Essential Guide to Depression.* New York: Pocket Books, 1998.

Smith, Douglas W. *Schizophrenia.* Danbury, CT: Franklin Watts, 1993.

Steel, Danielle. *His Bright Light: The Story of Nick Traina.* New York: Delacorte Publishing, 1998.

Torrey, E. Fuller. *Out of the Shadows: Confronting America's Mental Illness Crisis.* New York: John Wiley & Sons, Inc., 1996.

————. *Surviving Schizophrenia: A Manual for Families, Consumers and Providers,* 3rd ed. New York: HarperPerennial, 1995.

Woolis, Rebecca. *When Someone You Love Has a Mental Illness: A Handbook for Family, Friends, and Caregivers.* New York: J. P. Tarcher, 1992.

Wrobleski, Adina. *Suicide: Why? Eighty-Five Questions and Answers About Suicide, 2nd ed.* Mahtomedi, MN: SAVE, 1995.

Index

www.ingramcontent.com/pod-product-compliance
Lightning Source LLC
Chambersburg PA
CBHW050731030426
42336CB00012B/1511